T0248272

Simple Secrets to Becoming a Saving Whiz

Simple Secrets to Becoming a Saving Whiz

Stop Feeling Overwhelmed, Take Control of Your Money, and Create the Lifestyle You Want

Gina Zakaria

WILEY

Published by John Wiley & Sons, Inc., Hoboken, New Jersey.
Published simultaneously in Canada.

For general information on our other products and services or for technical support, please contact our Customer Care Department within the United States at (800) 762-2974, outside the United States at (317) 572-3993 or fax (317) 572-4002.

Wiley also publishes its books in a variety of electronic formats. Some content that appears in print may not be available in electronic formats. For more information about Wiley products, visit our web site at www.wiley.com.

Library of Congress Cataloging-in-Publication Data is Available:

ISBN 9781394195817 (Cloth)
ISBN 9781394195824 (ePub)
ISBN 9781394195831 (ePDF)

Cover Design: Wiley
Cover Image: © Anton Shaparenko/Adobe Stock
Author Photo: Courtesy of the Author

SKY10059891_111023

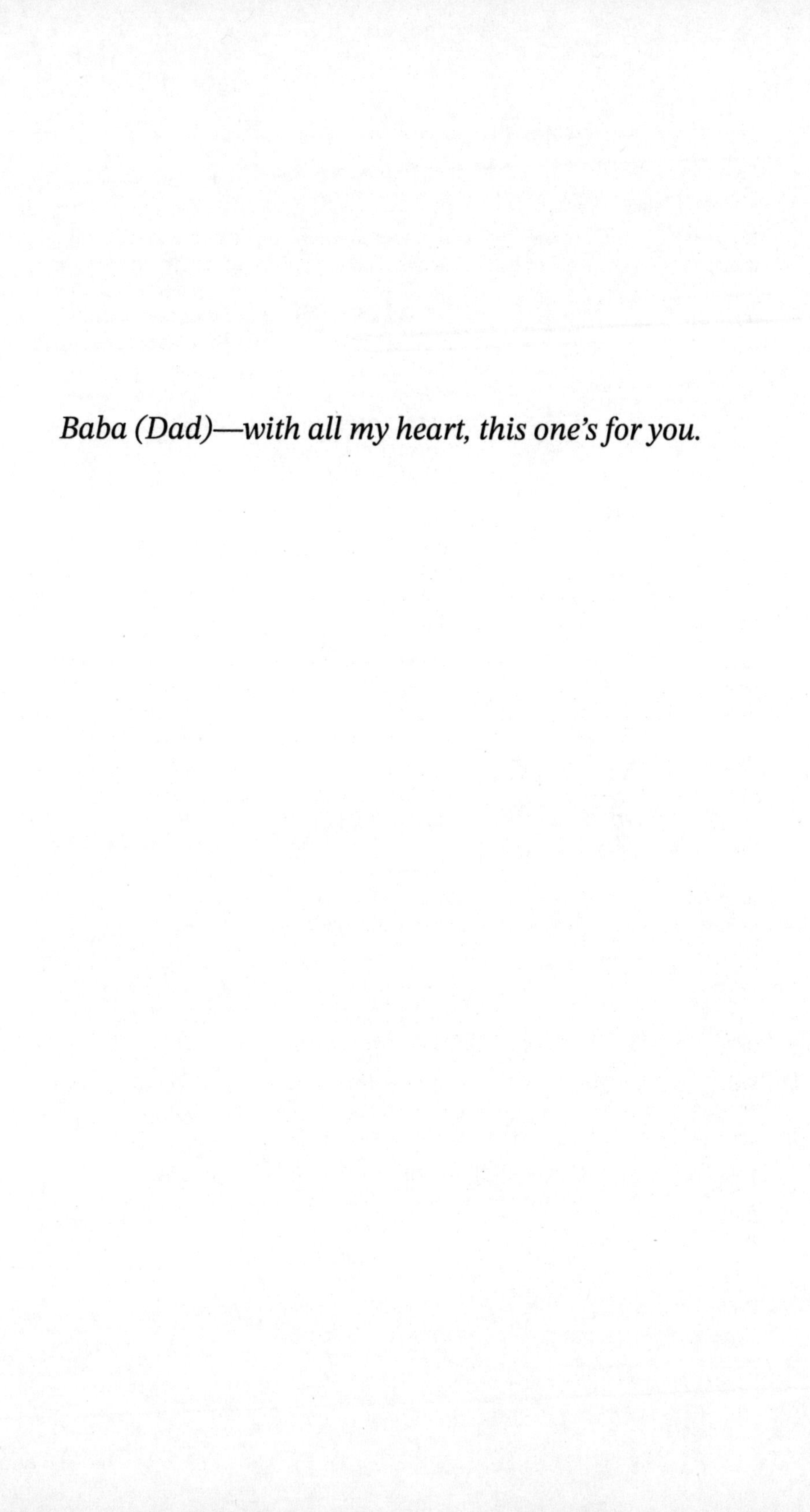

Baba (Dad)—with all my heart, this one's for you.

Contents

Acknowledgments

This book was only made possible because of a wonderful village of people who provided the space, guidance, support, and love to make it happen. I am so thankful to God for blessing me with this incredible opportunity to serve others in such an impactful way.

To my darling husband, Ashraf, your love and support knows no bounds. Thank you for your unwavering belief in me, for all the roles you assumed, to give me more time to write, and for the countless pep talks you gave me.

To my daughters, Sarah and Ashley, thank you for being my sounding board when I needed to think out loud, for being my cheerleaders every step of the way, and for being the true catalysts for fixing my financial life. Sarah, thank you for pushing me to start a blog. Your push led me to ultimately write this book, a childhood dream I never imagined coming true. Ashley, thank you for reminding me to take breaks when I was zoned in for hours.

To my mom, who always saw more in me than I could see in myself, whose prayers, patience, and love made all this possible. Your words and teachings will forever live in my heart and in this book.

To my Wiley team, you are the real MVPs. To Sally, who reached out and spoke life into my dream, thank you for believing in me. To Deborah and Kevin, thanks for your support during this entire process. To Kelly, a heartfelt thank-you for the loving care you put into this book, I couldn't have done this without your direction, guidance, and constant uplifting support.

To my friend, Dr. Brad Klontz, thank you for generously sharing your expertise, providing your guidance, and most of all for your friendship, which gave me the confidence and courage to write this book.

And finally, to you, the reader. Thank you, friend. Without you, this book wouldn't have been possible. Thank you for putting your faith in me and allowing me into your world by reading this book. I hope that it helps you make positive changes with your money and empowers you to keep moving forward.

Introduction

Fixing your finances can feel overwhelming and stressful. And if you've ever attempted to fix your finances on your own, you may have come across terms or concepts that added more confusion. Since money is a universal concept, it's important that it's universally understood. This book intends to simplify your money journey by breaking down the complicated concepts into easy-to-understand nuggets of knowledge so you can confidently take steps forward and make progress.

There are five major parts to this book. The first two parts ("Unlearn" and "Assess and Address") aim to help you recognize where you are, how you got there, and what to do to move forward with your finances. The last three parts ("Grocery Savings," "Bill Savings," and "Budget Better") offer practical approaches that help you sidestep common pitfalls and methods that can help you reach your financial goals with more ease. Each part has chapters that are intended to provide a deeper understanding of the overarching theme of that part.

It's important to mention a few things that make this book a bit different from your average personal finance book. First and foremost, while I do have a background in finance, I wrote this book from the point of view of an ordinary mom who wanted to fix her finances without sacrificing her lifestyle in the process. This book is very much a conversation from one friend to another about all the freedom that was discovered in keeping things simple. So you won't find me teaching you accounting techniques or financial formulas that require charts and spreadsheets to learn. Instead, I show you financial concepts and approaches that make your financial journey just a little bit easier and a lot less overwhelming.

Second, your personal finance journey is personal. This book is not meant to encompass every possible scenario or rare situations that require certain actions to be resolved but instead focuses on teaching thought-provoking principles that aim to shift your perspective and help transform your mindset over time. Whether you are a single mom with a high school diploma or a high-income singleton with a PhD, the principles and approaches highlighted in this book provide structure with the freedom to adapt the methods in a way that supports your personal money goals.

Third, this book is for educational purposes and is not to be taken as financial advice. Its intended purpose is to foster new perspective, shift your mindset, help you build healthier financial habits, and empower you to take charge of your financial health and life.

Are you ready to begin your journey to an easier, simpler life of financial freedom? Great! Let's get started.

Part I
Unlearn

Chapter 1
Big Goals Don't Budge

One message was crystal clear when I was a kid: big always meant better. I was always told to think big, dream big, and do big things. I didn't realize it at the time, but every interaction I had growing up pointed to the same underlying message: Success starts with a plan. A big plan. After all, big means better, doesn't it?

By the time I was in junior high school, I was expected to make big decisions too, like planning my future career path. And one night, as my mom and I were watching TV, I decided to share my big plan. I told her that I wanted to be a lawyer when I grew up. You see, being raised in an Egyptian home meant that there were essentially three acceptable career options to choose from: lawyer, doctor, or engineer. And to my excitement, my career choice landed right inside the parameters of what was acceptable. I'll never forget my mom's response when I shared my plan with her. It wasn't necessarily what she said that stuck with me as much as the message that the words carried. She said lovingly, "You'll be more than a lawyer; one day, you'll be a judge."

I'm certain that those words were meant to give me confidence and show my mom's support, more than anything. And while her words were motivating, it was the underlying message that subtly made its way into shaping my mindset. That day, I realized that my goals and plans were not big enough. They needed to be bigger. A goal had to feel scary for it to be worthwhile.

Fast-forward to college graduation; I earned a Bachelor of Science in business and never became a judge or even a lawyer for that matter. Along the way, I realized that the law field wasn't for me, but somehow, a part of me felt like I took the easy way out. Even though I graduated with honors in a field I loved, it still felt like I failed because a Bachelor of Science degree had nowhere near the prestige of a Juris Doctorate. My accomplishment didn't feel big enough. I shake my head as I think of this moment now, but back then, that “fail” shook my confidence.

I continued to carry the “big goal” mentality into adulthood until I found myself as an all-or-nothing type of doer. It affected every part of my life. I either cleaned the entire house from top to bottom, reorganizing every drawer and closet, or left the dishes in the sink and my socks on the floor for days.

Inevitably, this mindset made its way into my financial life as well. With every major money goal I created, failure would be lurking around the corner, just waiting for me. And with every failure came another big swing to knock down my self-confidence. My big goals began to feel more like a burden and less like the admirable ambition I once thought they were, until they eventually became a stumbling block that stopped me from getting ahead.

But things really came to a head when my husband and I had just purchased our first house and almost immediately decided to renovate it because how else would we make this house “our home”? We were big fans of home renovation shows at the time and believed that for our space to feel like us, we had to knock down walls, paint every corner, and buy new pieces to decorate the space. So we did just that and found ourselves in a whopping $106,000 of high-interest debt in a matter of months!

Fully Committing to the Big Goal Mindset

Feeling overwhelmed, I settled deeper into my comfort zone mindset and put my “big goals” cap on. Surely, I thought, this time would be different, and I had so many reasons to believe it would be. At this point, I was older, wiser, and had more drive to make it work. I convinced myself that it wasn't the "big goal" mindset that was the problem, but that I just had not been disciplined enough to make it work before. But now I was determined to get out of debt, so I decided to commit to sticking to the plan, and we'd become debt free in no time.

The big goal I created seemed to be quite simple, at least on the surface. Our goal was to pay off our debt by halting all our spending except to pay bills and necessities. My logic was that this would create a ton of savings, and all those savings would go toward paying off our debt. Sounds straightforward, right? What could possibly go wrong?

So my husband and I tried this plan out for a few months. But every month, without missing a beat, we'd fail. And you'd think that this would be a sign for me to reassess, but nope! In my stubborn determination to succeed this time, I kept trying again and again. I'd restart each month the same way, convinced that this month I would be more disciplined and focused to make it work. After all, I was certain that the problem was not in my goal but rather in my lack of discipline.

This went on for months until one morning, I was on the very edge of losing all my patience. That morning, I was up at 4:30 a.m. and started my 45-minute commute to work before the sun came out. As I was driving, I felt frustrated and resentful. Here I am driving to work, already in a bad mood and on payday for that matter! My frustration came from the utter exhaustion I'd felt up until this point. Every extra dollar from our paychecks was going toward our debt payments, yet it felt like we were progressing at a snail's pace. Every dollar that paid debt should have felt motivating, but instead it felt depleting. Looking at our total debt, it seemed like we were not making much progress, even though we were sacrificing so much and gave ourselves no room for any fun. No takeout, no outings, no breaks. It was exhausting and draining, and it wasn't realistic for us to continue carrying on this way. There was no way we could sustain this plan long term, and I was ready to give up. But in that moment of frustration and hopelessness, I had a moment of clarity. "This plan sucks," I thought. "It's not *me* who's failing the plan; *the plan* is failing me!"

Shifting the Perspective to Achieve the Goal

My plan had failed, and I was frustrated. Why was my big goal so hard to accomplish? Why did big goals continue to stunt my progress? From where I was standing, it seemed like everyone else had the ability to reach their big goals. So what did they know that I didn't? As I dug deeper trying to find answers, I discovered a major flaw in big goals that changed my perspective.

If your eyes are solely on the big goal, it will always feel like you're not making progress. Imagine you're on a road trip and you need to travel past some mountains in the distance. If you focus your gaze on the mountains, no matter how much you drive, they still seem far away, and you have the illusion that you're not moving toward them.

But if you keep your foot on the gas and focus on the road in front of you instead of the mountains, you'll start to keep track of every mile driven, noticing your progress when you've driven five miles, then ten, and then fifty. Then, when you periodically take your eyes off the road and look back up at the mountains, you'll realize how much closer you are. Those miles seem like small steps when you're driving, yet they make all the difference in your journey to reach the mountains.

That's what I had been missing all along. I had been focusing on the mountains instead of the miles. After years of being conditioned to keep my eye on my big goals, I had to first shift my perspective to focus on the true driver of success, which is the steps along the way. This shift was the key factor that would eventually change my mindset and my approach.

Recognizing the Limitations of Big Goals

With so many success stories we see on social media, publications, and the news, we're inadvertently led to believe that big goals are the standalone plan to achieve great accomplishments. That's not the way success works, for anyone. Sure, creating big goals reflects ambition, drive, and the belief that you can make them happen. But are we creating big goals merely to feel good about having them or to accomplish the positive changes we want to make?

The reality is that big goals don't conform to practicality. If you don't have practical and realistic steps, then every failure feels extremely personal. You begin to question your ability to follow through, and you'll lose confidence in yourself. Even though on the surface they seem harmless, they're almost always accompanied by feelings of being stressed, overwhelmed, stuck. Big goals don't motivate; they intimidate.

This is especially true for big goals set in our financial life. Success requires progress, and progress requires focusing on the small steps that push you forward. When we solely focus on big goals without breaking them down into action steps, we often feel stuck and overwhelmed by the sheer size of them.

Feeling overwhelmed is a direct result of trying to do too much too fast. We lose momentum when we try to take big leaps. Instead, we need to focus on small steps to create the rhythm of progress that we seek.

Think of it this way: If you're currently living paycheck to paycheck, would it be reasonable to expect you to pay off all your debt, save six months' worth of living expenses just because you made it a goal? How about building wealth? Can you realistically build your wealth at a time when you're currently staring at the last seven dollars and fifty-six cents available in your checking account? The idea that somehow creating big goals results in achieving them, as if through some type of osmosis, is silly. Big goals are simply not enough to foster big change, at least not on their own.

Redefining Big Goals and Putting Them in Their Proper Place

Big goals are not the end-all, be-all of the planning process for our finances. This isn't to say that big goals are inherently wrong and that you should ditch them altogether. But they don't lead you to success on their own. To achieve a big goal, you need to focus on the steps and structure needed to make progress. For big goals to work correctly in driving us to success, they need to be redefined.

The irony that small steps take you further than big goals is not lost on me. Small steps seem to be the underdogs of financial planning, and for that reason, they're often overlooked. Yet the power that they hold is much greater in pushing you forward in your financial progress. Once you give them their true position in your plan, you'll discover just how much impact they create. Small steps are overachievers in every sense of the word. They take that great big overwhelming goal, break it down to a structured road map that you can easily follow, and help you go from zero to hero with your finances, without taking drastic measures that disrupt your life. They are exactly what you need if you want to achieve your financial goals in a way that is sustainable. And arguably the best part of small steps is that they do all their work quietly, without much chaos or commotion, and without being loud and pretentious, like their counterparts tend to be. People around you probably won't even notice them working, but you'll soon recognize how they begin to radically transform your financial life and, with that, your mindset too.

Chapter 2
The Magic Power of Small Steps

I'm a checklist-type of person. My checklists keep me organized, hold me accountable, and remind me of all the things I want to complete. Checklists also help me transfer my thoughts into action steps. But I often find that I ignore the hard tasks and instead scan my list for the easiest tasks to do first. By the time I finish the easy tasks, I've almost completely depleted my energy, and the bigger items move to the following day's list. Sadly, there are times when I don't get to the bigger items for a week or more, and when I do finally start to work on them, I've built up so much anxiety toward the tasks that they feel ten times harder to complete.

This happens with financial tasks as well, such as paying off debt, purchasing a home, or even achieving a job promotion. The bigger the tasks, the more we convince ourselves that we need more time to prepare for it, so we continue putting it off and procrastinating. Before we realize what's happening, that task has been pushed back weeks, months, and sometimes years.

The irony is that these big tasks are important and usually would greatly improve our financial functionality and, in turn, our life. These tasks need our attention, but their complexity and/or size causes us to hesitate, defer, and avoid them altogether. But as discussed in Chapter 1, "Big Goals Don't Budge," big goals can feel overwhelming, which causes us to doubt if we can accomplish them. We avoid that uncomfortable feeling through completing tasks that are easier, lighter, and quicker to finish. Those tasks give us the dopamine hit we seek, as we proudly check things off the list while simultaneously avoiding the harder items. But our avoidance here is telling us something important. It reveals that our big tasks are too complicated. And instead of recognizing this, we try to push through the hard items anyway.

Let me first be clear: There is no doubt that you can do hard things. But, if there's an easier way, why would you intentionally choose the harder way? Will it matter whether you took one big leap versus five small jumps, if in the end you still arrive at the same distance? No, it's the distance that matters, not how you got there.

Divide and Conquer

It's as simple as this: We need to break down our big tasks to make them easier to complete. It's the "divide and conquer" strategy. Typically used in war or political agendas, this strategy works on breaking larger groups into smaller ones to weaken them and, in turn, control or conquer them. And by controlling and conquering one small group at a time, eventually the entire group is conquered.

This strategy is effective in simplifying our finances as well. As each large task is broken down into several smaller steps, you'll be able to complete each step easier, bringing you one step closer to completing the entire task.

Imagine what this strategy can do for your debt payoff goals. When my husband and I were paying off our six figures of debt, this strategy made it easier to make progress and stay on track. Here are some of the steps that helped us:

- We consolidated some of our balances onto a card that had a 0% APR promotion for 12 months.
- We used what's known as the "avalanche method" to organize our debt payments. With the avalanche method, you list debt from highest interest rate to lowest interest rate. You make the largest possible payment to the first debt on the list while

making the minimum payments to all other debt. Continue until you work your way down the list and pay off all debt.

- We saved money on the small, everyday expenses, like groceries and gas, and put those savings toward the first debt.

Each step built on the previous one. As we saved money on groceries, even if it was twenty dollars, we added it to our debt payment. As months went by, we started paying more of our debt, which eventually shortened our list of debts. A shorter list meant that we didn't have as many minimum payments to make, and that extra money could pay off the first debt on our list. This created positive momentum and gave us the small wins we needed to keep making progress.

Small steps have a lot of power, and that power compounds your effort over time. They also eliminate anxiety by simplifying the process and giving you an easier road map to follow.

But to fully embrace the use of small steps, you first need to abandon the tendency to take extreme measures. That's a strategy that often accompanies the "big step" approach, and it just doesn't serve you well. For example, you might decide to cut out fast food altogether to lose weight; get rid of fifty percent of your things to keep your house tidy; or strip all the fun from your budget and spending plan to save money. Steps like these are too hard to sustain and simply don't last long enough to take root in your routine.

Drastic measures polish the surface but don't provide a deep clean to your habits, routines, and mindset. They are not effective in deeper, longer-lasting transformative change.

Sure, these steps might work for a day, a week, maybe even a month if you're really committed. But deprivation is not a long-term solution. Small steps get you to your goal too, without pushing you beyond your limits. And that creates a healthy road to financial recovery.

Mastering a Budget

I was anti-budget for years; I absolutely loathed the idea. My husband, who's an accountant by trade (and by passion), would try so hard to convince me that we needed one, but it was a hard "no" for me. At the time, I thought of a budget as a big, drastic change that was defined as restriction, deprivation, and penny pinching. Erm, no, thank you!

But not having a budget led to constant overspending, living paycheck to paycheck, and not having any control over our money. Eventually, I reluctantly gave in and created a budget with my husband that helped us buy our first house and afford our new mortgage. But my husband managed most of it. The second time around, I had to be a more active participant. So we created another budget plan that would help us pay off debt and create financial stability in our lives. I still wasn't sold on the whole budgeting thing, but it was time to put my feelings aside and get serious about our money.

Since I was already hesitant, I didn't want to jump in head first. So, instead, I decided to break down every part of the budgeting process to make it easier on me. I first reviewed every expense line that I was responsible for. We agreed that my husband would handle the fixed expenses, and I would handle the variable expenses. My group included groceries, gas, gifts, takeout, entertainment, memberships, and the like. Incidentally, these were also the expenses that needed the most work, as our fixed expenses were in good shape.

I took time to learn ways I could reduce these expenses. I read books, blogs, and articles, listened to podcasts, and watched YouTube videos, and I started making a list of steps to try. Some steps worked well while others didn't, and I found that the steps that worked the best had one common trait. They were small. Each small action step felt easy and doable. And because they were small, they didn't take much time to complete. And every time I completed a task, I saw results that gave me motivation to take another step. Up until this point, a budget felt hard and drastic, but applying small steps made it feel kind of like a game. It felt . . . fun. Within a few months, I was consistently reducing costs and saving money, and we were paying off debt faster and faster. It was exhilarating!

Small Builds Momentum

Small steps were exactly what I needed to master my budget. Small steps provided simplicity for me, and that is where I found clarity, gained control, and built confidence. It created the solid foundation necessary to achieve big goals.

But "simple" can sound unappealing to some people. It sounds too much like a shortcut, too easy, too small. It doesn't feel ambitious enough, and thus, not an admirable way to do things. It almost feels like the lazy way out, like an underdog of goal setting.

People often associate the term "small" with words like deficient, inadequate, slight, puny, stunted, and even stingy. Those descriptions don't sound exciting or inspiring. These words scream, "You're not doing enough!"

And perhaps that's why so many people go in the opposite direction toward "big goals." Big goals come with a type of reputation that's appealing. Implementing plans that are big, great, and grand feels better to the ego. But while "big" gets the respect, "small" gets the job done and helps you to the finish line.

"Small" is a fierce yet subtle beast, and it prevails in everything you do. I bet you haven't noticed many of the small steps that have brought you to where you are now. Take a moment to think about your current financial situation. How much debt do you have? How much money do you have saved up or invested? How much, in total, have you paid for streaming services in the last seven years? Do the math, I'll wait. Now, look at those totals and ask yourself this question, how many of these happened overnight?

I'm going to take a wild guess and say none of them. Every single number you have in your financial portfolio, good or bad, resulted from hundreds or even thousands of tiny, seemingly insignificant decisions that you made daily, and these decisions added up over the span of years.

Imagine that your car breaks down. You don't currently have a budget or spending plan, so you haven't consistently saved for emergencies. Or maybe you have a budget, but it didn't include an emergency fund. As of right now, most of your paycheck goes to bills, and the rest is divided between some essentials and lifestyle luxuries, so there's never any money left over to save. So how do you pay for your car repairs? You charge them to your credit card.

Adding repair costs to your existing debt resulted from a series of small, subtle decisions and action steps you took over time. Each choice you made directly had an impact on the current situation.

The Domino Theory

A single result is rarely ever the product of one big decision or action. Rather, everything we do is a series of small actions over time. This is the effect of the "Domino Theory," as described and adopted by Herb Morreale (Computer Science Industry Advisor, University of Colorado, Boulder) in 2002. Morreale explains, "All it takes is one small strategic action to set big things in motion and align with the actions of others."

This is the unseen power of small action steps. And as you've discovered a little earlier in this chapter, you've been practicing this theory in every part of your life.

Think about how you cook your meals. When was the last time you dumped everything in your pot and walked away? Creating a delicious meal requires a recipe (or method), and that recipe includes many smaller steps. Most professional chefs start their dish preparation with a "mise en place." It's a French phrase translated as "setting in place, positioning," which is a culinary process in which ingredients are prepared and organized before cooking. Each ingredient is washed, prepped, and measured so it's ready to add into the pot at the right time, in a specific order. It's the process of small steps that builds up the flavor in a dish.

According to Morreale, you only need to topple a few dominoes to start a process that eventually knocks down a final domino that is many times greater in mass than the first domino. By giving every small step the space to do its work, we are essentially putting in motion smaller dominoes that build such force that they can knock down a much more important domino at the end. That domino is your much larger goal.

Don't underestimate the power that small steps provide. They are small but mighty when it comes to the impact they create. The power of small steps is undeniable when you think of how they have already impacted your life. And now that you know their power, tapping into it will be a game changer for your financial success.

Chapter 3
A Spoonful of Consistency and a Dash of Patience

It's not enough to *know* that small steps are powerful. Knowing what works doesn't magically change anything. What creates change is how you apply the knowledge. More so, the mindset with which you apply that knowledge is what ultimately determines the level of success you reach.

Interestingly, your mindset either makes or breaks your progress. So if we're conditioned with a mindset that's centered on the idea that speed equals efficiency, then adopting small steps will feel like we're not doing enough. And that feeling can cause us to quit before we see any progress.

Fast Often Fails

We see this play out a lot in the weight loss space. Let's illustrate this with a typical dieter, and let's call her Rachel. Rachel has been dieting on and off for 20 years, and she has tried almost every popular - fad diet. She's gotten so good at dieting that she even knows how many calories an apple or an orange are, from memory. She knows all the basic principles to weight loss and understands that losing one-half pound to one pound per week is a healthy rate. But in the 20 years of her weight loss journey, she hasn't successfully lost weight and kept it off.

So if she has all this knowledge of how weight loss works, why hasn't she permanently lost weight yet?

To answer this, we need to look at Rachel's weight loss cycle. She typically starts a new diet plan every time she's feeling fed up with the number on the scale. She doesn't like how she looks in any of her clothes and finds herself struggling to apply nail polish to her toes, put lotion on her feet, or just tie her shoes in the morning. A tinge of desperation permeates the air every time she faces her closet full of clothes that no longer fit, and she hates the idea of buying new clothes in this bigger size.

This is precisely when she decides it's time for a major change . . . again. Her plan is usually the same every time: She'll start a new diet on Monday and get rid of any tempting foods she has at home. In preparation, she buys all the "healthy foods," such as chicken breast, fruits, and vegetables to make healthy meals. She also decides to dust off her yoga mat and go back to the gym five days a week, no exceptions. She is determined to make this time the last time.

Sound familiar? Let's keep going to see what happens next.

Monday comes, and she's ready! She wakes up early, puts on her gym clothes, and heads to the gym. She works out for an hour and heads home to get ready for work. Her breakfast of overnight oats and veggie-packed salad for lunch were prepared the night before, so she puts them in her lunch bag and heads to work. After work she goes home and prepares her healthy dinner. She finishes dinner and preps tomorrow's lunch. Tomorrow is just like today; everything is repeated in hopes that it becomes a solid routine and lifestyle. After all, she has read that it takes 21 days to form a habit, so she is determined to get to 21 days before having any cheat meals. Sounds like a good enough plan, right?

So, again we ask, what makes her fail? From an outsider looking in, it's crystal clear. She's doing too much, too fast. First, she went from having no structure to a rigid structure, literally overnight. Second, she made several changes at once, adding unnecessary mental pressure. Third, she adopted the all-or-nothing approach. She went from eating what she wants, to cutting out all the things she loves and plans to restrict herself from eating those foods for at least three weeks.

Naturally, what do you think is going to happen when she crosses the three-week threshold? It's very likely that she'll overindulge on her favorite foods and hate herself in the morning, resulting in even more restriction to make up for what she ate yesterday.

This is a cycle of failure! And while this isn't an actual case study because I am not an expert on the matter of weight or nutrition, nor did I interview a study sample to draw these conclusions, I am qualified to draw them. Why? Because like many people, I was Rachel.

Time Is Essential

I lived this scenario for over 20 years, and I can wholeheartedly say that it never once worked for the long term. What's worse is every fail felt personal—failing meant I wasn't strong enough, didn't have enough willpower, or just didn't have what it took to be successful. My perspective didn't change until my doctor explained that lasting change takes years. Years! With weight loss, your body needs time to catch up to your weight, otherwise, it will fight to pack on the pounds again. For your body to adjust and sustain weight loss, it needs years of reprogramming your habits and building consistent routines that replace your old ones.

Similarly, your finances need time to evolve too. Perhaps it won't take years, but it will take time. Time gives your habits the space they need to gradually solidify into a system that fosters your financial growth. A quick fix fades out before this process even begins. That's why fad diets come and go. They don't have the longevity to survive.

If you look at your current financial habits, you'll find that they formed over time. It probably took months and even years for those habits to form. Healthy financial habits will also take time because they're transforming the distorted picture and creating a completely new outlook. Just as cement needs to be molded and shaped before allowing it to cure, we must take the time to mold and shape our new habits so that when they are made solid, they serve us well.

The best thing you can give to your financial goals is time. Small steps need time to make a noticeable impact. So how do we give our goals enough time to thrive without feeling discouraged?

A Powerful Duo

Meet Consistency and Patience. They're the nerds behind the glam of success! No one likes talking about them because they have a reputation for being the boring part of the journey. But they are key to creating harmony with small steps, time, and you. That harmony creates a momentum that is powerful.

You might have tried patience and consistency with your financial goals before, but you might not have been able to really vibe with them because they don't fit in with fast-paced timelines. You know, the timelines we see all over the place that other people seem to effortlessly crush?

Zoomed-in Pictures Lie

If you read somewhere that Susan paid off a million dollars of debt in just two years or that Sally 10X'd her wealth in 12 months, naturally you'd want to reach your goals just as fast, right?

Well Susan, paid off most of her million-dollar debt by selling her home and the rest was a result of budgeting and saving money, a discipline she learned over time. And Sally only started 10X-ing her wealth after five years of consistently contributing to her investment accounts with every paycheck. This isn't said to minimize their success story, but it's critical that we take a step back to see the entire picture. What most of us don't see is that overnight success never happens overnight; it takes months and sometimes years.

And plans that promise super-fast results often require unreasonable amounts of sacrifice and deprivations, sacrifices like banning yourself from ever stepping foot into a restaurant, cutting out meat for most of your dinners, saving over 50% of your take home salary by pinching pennies on everything, and never paying for entertainment. I don't know about you, but to me, it all just sounds so . . . restrictive.

And let me be clear, there are many people who are happily living this type of life, and you may be one of them. And if that's the case, keep on doing what works for you. But I'm guessing that you're reading this book either because you've tried that method in the past and it failed you or you read this type of advice and, like me, were repulsed by it.

This is not to say that sacrificing for your goals is inherently wrong. On the contrary, every goal requires a certain degree of discipline and habit changes to be successful. But it's important to find the right balance that works for you long-term so you can sustain the change.

The Philosophy of Time

When my husband and I set out to fix our finances and ditch debt, we wanted long-lasting change, and deprivation was not our vibe.

So we set out to create a path to debt freedom that would work with our season of life, our income level, and our priorities. At the time, our kids were only twelve and seven. We weren't willing to put their lives on hold while we fixed our finances.

Instead, we sought to find a balance we could live with, one that helped us reach our goals and allowed us to enjoy time with our kids while they were still children. It took us a little under five years to pay off over $106,000 of debt. When we were in the thick of it, it felt like it was taking forever, but looking back now, it's already been five years since our debt-free date, and that feels like it flew by! Time is constant, but it's our mindset that makes things seem to go fast or slow.

> *"Dripping water hollows out stone, not through force but through persistence."*
>
> *—Ovid*

Think about how dripping water is so small that it's not even called a trickle. It's a tiny, insignificant amount of water that has no real power on its own. It doesn't even have enough power to quench someone's thirst. Seems almost useless when you think about it like that. But when those drips, so small and weak, are combined with time and consistency, something magical happens. The drops amplify in strength and eventually cut through stone. Stone, an element that seems virtually unbreakable, is defeated by droplets of water, over time.

Sounds miraculous! But it's not surprising. Time amplifies small steps, and if we can practice patience, we can allow time to do its magic. It gives you the space you need to gradually build your habits with ease. It also gives you clarity so you can adjust as you go and make subtle changes that don't flip your life upside down. It also eliminates the stress that often comes with trying to finish fast.

And time does its best work with consistency. Consistency takes each small step and gives it the energy to continue moving forward. Isaac Newton's first law of motion describes the principle of inertia and says, "An object in motion remains in motion at constant speed and in a straight line unless acted on by an unbalanced force." Let's break it down so we can apply it to our financial steps. The principle of inertia describes that an "object" (small step) "remains in motion" (continues to work) "at constant speed and in a straight line" (consistently) unless an "unbalanced force" disrupts it (you stop repeating the small step).

By this theory, we can see that small steps continue to work consistently unless you stop repeating the steps. The operative word here is "you." You control the level of consistency. When you're regularly taking small steps, you build an inertia that completely transforms your finances. And that constant forward motion creates a momentum that's unstoppable.

It All Works Together

Time, patience, consistency, and small steps rely on each other to perform up to their full potential and serve your financial goals well. Committing to them helps you achieve incredible success! And that builds confidence to keep you moving forward and leveling up with your finances.

With all that said, practicing patience and consistency (ironically) takes time. It's not realistic to expect that you'll magically become patient and consistent with your goals. You still must do the work in shifting your habits and mindset gradually until these attributes become woven into the fabric of your routines. And this type of shift requires a much more active approach to change. To learn how to be more patient and consistent, we must first unlearn what we've been taught about conquering goals, especially when it comes to timelines.

Ditch the Timelines

Timelines have been folded into the standard of success in a way we can't ignore. Every milestone has been tagged with a specific timeline, whether that be a certain age, number of months, or dollar amount. By twenty-five years old, you should own a home; by the age of thirty, you should make a six-figure salary. By the age of forty, you should have at least one million dollars saved for retirement. These are just a few of the milestone timelines we've heard thrown around on social media, in social settings, and even in well-known publications—think about lists like 30 Under 30.

It's no wonder that in today's world, it can be quite a challenge to go from "microwave" patience to "slow cooker" patience. We've been programmed to believe that success is measured by time. So when we achieve a goal later than some societally imposed timeline, it often feels a little shameful that somehow, we're less than others who met that goal sooner. And while you may think you're a patient person (and you might be right), I challenge you to take a moment and think of how you feel waiting for your phone or laptop to load a page that takes an extra few seconds or when you're waiting for a stop light to turn green on the way to work.

This is precisely why it's important to be mindful as we reprogram our mindset to accept patience as an integral part of the process of success. You may find it helpful to take away timelines altogether in the beginning and then reintroduce timelines as you strengthen your patience muscle. For the time being, focus on the steps you plan to implement. For example, if your goal is to save money on groceries, start with "I will cook one pantry meal per week" instead of "I will save X amount of money per week." Focus on the task instead of the arbitrary numbers. The tasks eventually get you to the desired number anyway.

When I first started saving money on groceries, I didn't set a goal to save a certain amount or set a timeline. I was not dedicated enough at the time to expect a specific outcome. Instead, I made one small change at a time. The first small step I took was reviewing my sales ads weekly. That goal resulted in me picking which grocery store to shop at each week, which resulted in saving money. My one task of checking the ads led to achieving my main target goal. Focus on the task at hand and do it consistently and trust the plan.

To summarize, small changes paired with consistency and patience deliver massive success. But they require you to commit to follow through. None of this works unless you do.

Part II

Assess and Address

Chapter 4
You've Done This Before, Now Do It with Intention

My mom worked as a quality control inspector in the fashion industry for over thirty years before she retired. Her division was in charge of making sure that all garments met top quality standards before being shipped to the larger department stores. One of her tasks was to inspect the sewing quality of the pieces. Every day, she would drive to half a dozen factories, physically inspecting each garment to ensure that the stitching was accurately sewn. She spent several hours per day on this task, which required a keen eye for detail and a relentless determination to meet a near-perfect quality standard on a consistent basis. This particular task became more than a mere job duty for my mom; it became the standard by which she measured the quality of every piece of clothing we personally purchased and owned.

When my mom and I would shop for my clothing at places such as Urban Outfitters, Charlotte Russe, and Forever 21 in my teen years, she'd always come with me to the fitting room, not to judge the style or fit of the piece, but to check the stitching. To her and my disappointment, most pieces did not meet her standards. It would take us hours to find acceptable pieces, and when I'd get frustrated in the process, she'd remind me that stitching, a seemingly insignificant detail, one that most people often overlooked, was a vital component to the longevity of that article of clothing. When done correctly, the article of clothing can last decades, but when done incorrectly, it might not last through dinner (#wardrobemalfunction).

While I hated the process growing up, I've learned to appreciate the trade secrets my mom shared with me, and to this day I meticulously search for good quality pieces, just like my mom taught me.

Your Intentionality Matters

Good quality clothing is made with the intention to last. And that intention is shown through the seams of the garment. Every seam is made up of small, repetitive stitching that creates a stunning piece. Every stitch directs the fabric to lay a certain way, accentuates ideal shapes while hiding imperfections, and gives the wearer peace of mind in its durability, trusting that everything that's meant to be covered, stays covered.

Style, coverage, durability, peace of mind. All these rely on one . . . simple . . . stitch. It's small yet incredibly powerful in its functionality.

Every single stitch is essentially one small step in the final creation of the piece. There are thousands of tiny stitches throughout a garment, but it only takes one weak stitch to ruin the entire piece.

That's also how simple steps work when it comes to our finances. Simple steps are, by nature, small, but they have always been an integral component in forming our habits and creating our financial results. These steps act as the stitching that brings our entire financial "garment" to life. And what's wild is that, without realizing it, we've been using simple steps in our finances all along.

Shocking, right? Many of the outcomes we're currently facing in our financial life are a result of a series of small steps we mindlessly took at one point in time. Without noticing, those small steps compounded over time and inadvertently created what my mom would call a "low quality stitch" on our financial garment. That weak stitch was destined to unravel at some point and expose our financial vulnerability at the most inopportune time.

This unraveling shows up through debt, out-of-control spending, living paycheck to paycheck, and so on.

The Proof Is in the Stitching

And as we inspect the stitching of our current financial situation, we can start to easily spot the weak stitches that caused it all to unravel. Our small steps (as inconsequential as they may have seemed) eventually had quite a noticeable impact.

The truth is, small steps can make or break your finances, and we've seen those unfortunate events play out many times in the media. Ever wonder why some people who make over six figures in salary per year are living paycheck to paycheck and feel financially stuck? Or how others (e.g., celebrities) who make millions of dollars per year "suddenly" find themselves on the brink of bankruptcy? It seems like it's always a shocker when we hear these stories about seemingly "rich" people struggling with money.

What about our financial situation? When you think of where you are now, did your hardship or struggle appear out of the blue? Most of us view our financial circumstance as a surprising discovery, as if somewhere along the line we somehow lost control suddenly and landed in this situation. However, if we dig deeper beyond the surface, it is clear that it was not a sudden change that took place but a much more gradual change.

The idea that our finances can change overnight is a complete myth. Financial transformation (positive or negative) takes time to develop and doesn't occur all of a sudden. Drastic change doesn't usually happen drastically. Sometimes it may seem unexpected if you aren't paying attention to the signs, but every drastic change is made up of many tiny decisions. Those tiny decisions feel miniscule compared to the grand scheme of your finances, but those are the small stitches that form the fabric of your financial health.

Think about all the small steps and decisions we make every day and how they compound over the span of a week, a month, a year, or even a decade. Small, seemingly innocent purchases such as buying coffee every morning, grabbing a vending machine snack during your break, or buying lunch every day at work accumulate quickly and many times morph into slightly bigger actions, such as twenty dollars spent at Target or a twenty-five-dollar Amazon cart purchase (so you save on shipping cost). And those decisions unintentionally become the gateway for even bigger and more frequent spending habits. By the end of the month, we discover that we spent hundreds of dollars without even realizing it. But the bank statement clearly shows just how fast our mindless actions can add up to a disastrous amount of spending. Imagine what months two, three, and four might look like if we aren't careful.

This is how financial issues are created. No one ever intends for these small actions to get out of control, but they compound like wildfire.

This is why we must not underestimate the power of small steps by taking them lightly. Overlooking their power can lead to misusing them and having an adverse effect on our finances, as many of us have either experienced personally or watched someone close to us experience. So we need to be intentional with our use of small steps to avoid this major pitfall and instead make progress toward our financial goals.

The good news is that the compounding effect of small steps works in the opposite direction too. In other words, it's time to use small steps and watch them multiply and compound to your advantage.

Creating Your Simple Step Plan

The great thing about creating a financial plan that only uses small steps is how easy it is to start. It eliminates the extra pressure we often feel when we approach a new plan, which usually comes from trying to figure it all out at once. Instead, the simple steps ease us into taking action slowly. A simple step plan also has added flexibility, so you have freedom to adjust and adapt your steps based on how your priorities change. And this adaptability is what makes them easily sustainable in your life. Remember, our goal is to have long-lasting results that stand the test of time, and this only happens when our steps are so consistent that they become part of our routine. And the health of your routine is vital for the health of your finances.

Let's say you want to reach a goal of $10,000 saved for emergencies. For the purposes of this book, we are not creating a timeline, just a simple goal. With this goal in mind, your simple step plan might look like this:

1. Check last month's bank statement, highlighting each expense type and adding up their totals (your current spending rate).
2. Create a budget that reflects your current spending rate.
3. Add your new emergency savings fund to your savings section in your budget.
4. Open a new savings account and name it: "Emergencies."
5. For your budget, make sure your entire paycheck is divided among all your planned expenses.
6. Check that your income minus expenses equals zero at the end of your budget cycle (getting to zero means you've successfully directed every dollar of your paycheck and planned out your spending).

7. Start with one expense line to improve, like your grocery budget.
8. Research easy ways to save money on groceries.
9. Pick one money-saving grocery tip to try this week.
10. As you save money, add it to your new emergency savings account.
11. Track your savings every week.
12. Repeat step eight and nine until you've mastered step seven's line item.
13. Go back and repeat step seven.

Your plan might not look exactly like this, but this gives you a good idea of the simplicity of each step and provides a guide of some sort to help you create plans for other areas of your finances.

The list might seem like it was created for "dummies," obnoxiously obvious or so basic that it should be common sense. That's precisely the point and the beauty of keeping things simple! The steps are broken down to make them so easy that they're a no-brainer to complete. No-brainers are great because they provide quick wins that boost dopamine levels and make you feel good as you accomplish them. And in general, we are much more likely to complete tasks that don't require much of our time and attention. We already have too many things that compete for these limited resources, so having one task that can be done without much effort is eagerly welcomed.

As we've discussed at length in previous chapters, when we overcomplicate the process by creating "big" steps, especially at the beginning of our money journey, it creates a barrier for us, and it naturally repels us from moving forward. So, to avoid this obstacle, we procrastinate, which unfortunately stalls our progress and creates an added layer of pressure because now we think we're behind. A simple step plan is a much more effective approach to your finances. Implementing simple steps is like viewing your goals through a magnifying lens: it allows you to hyper-focus on one small part of the object at a time.

As you create your step-by-step plan, it's important to be mindful of where you are today and where you want to be tomorrow, nothing further than that. Most people tend to focus on the long term with the belief that this will help them have better focus and be more strategic. My husband fits within this camp of thinking and often quotes a well-known Arabic idea that says, "Mat bosesh taht riglek, bos oddam" (written in English letters with Arabic pronunciation). This loosely translates as "Don't look under your feet but look forward," meaning don't focus on the short term, focus on the long term. He uses this phrase often when he refers to a game of chess, a major life decision, or when talking about retirement strategies in the span of 10–20 years into the future. Since he works in the finance space and already has his small step plan in place, this way of thinking motivates and inspires him to make certain financial moves.

But for the purposes of this book (which is to help you build momentum, so you make progress without being overwhelmed), we're going to reverse the order of direction. Instead of focusing on the long term when you're just starting, keep your eyes on your feet, don't get distracted (or overwhelmed) by what's ahead. For our purposes, looking directly in front of you keeps your focus on the very next step, and that's what is needed to move forward.

It is more beneficial to focus on what we are capable of accomplishing in the moment instead of focusing on what we wish to accomplish far into the future. For example, if you want to save $100,000 in the next few years, focus on how much you can save today. It's the $20 that you save consistently that eventually increases to $100 and then $1,000, and eventually gets you to your $100,000 savings goal.

First crawl, then walk, then run. Master one phase at a time before moving on to the next phase of your journey.

The Smaller, the Better

There is a reason behind taking things one small step at a time. One of the main purposes behind applying simple steps is to eliminate, or at the very least, significantly minimize feeling overwhelmed, which tends to strike right before we're about to face a challenge. So creating a plan with super small steps is key. The smaller the step, the easier and quicker you can move forward to the next step in your plan. Even a simple step such as watching one YouTube video a day to learn how to save money on groceries is considered a step forward. By watching a video, you are still actively working on your goal, and that active step makes room for you to take another step forward. Remember, every step builds on the previous one, so you only need to focus on taking one step today that makes tomorrow's step easier. For instance, if you decide to clean your kitchen tonight and thaw out meat for tomorrow's dinner, then tomorrow, it will be that much easier to prepare dinner for your family, which in turn, saves you money by eating at home.

When you begin creating your steps, focus on breaking down each step to its most basic level. When you think you've broken it down far enough, break it down one more time. Yes, I'm willing to bet that the step can be broken down more. The step should be so small that you can complete it in one day. Here are a few examples:

- Check your grocery sale ads.
- Wash your dishes after dinner.
- Prep tomorrow's lunch.
- Save all your five-dollar bills.
- Call your Internet service provider and ask for a discount.

Super small and super simple. Each one requires minimal effort, so there is no barrier to get through the task, even on your busiest days.

Compounding Your Steps

As you practice completing small steps every day, you'll notice something magical happening. You'll become much more intentional with the steps you create. While at first, you just need to create small steps (any steps to get you started), you'll notice that your steps start to form a pattern with a natural progression. Each step will work in harmony to build on the previous step and support the following step.

Over time, your small steps become easier to execute while simultaneously compounding their impact on your end goal. So it gets easier while also accelerating your results? Seems too good to be true, right? That's the beauty of compounding. When you use it with intention, it can do the heavy lifting for you, and you can reach your goals with much more ease.

Chapter 5
Your Steps Matter

When I was six years old, I saw a television commercial about a new toy called the Popples Moon Hopper. It was basically a ball with a plastic platform around the middle that you could stand on and bounce. It kind of looked like the planet Saturn if the rings were attached to the planet and created a disk all the way around. Every kid I knew either had one or wanted one. So I asked my dad if we could go and buy one, and he said yes but that I'd have to wait one minute before we could go. So I counted to one and said, "Okay, let's go." He chuckled and told me that a minute is sixty seconds and I needed to count to sixty before we could go. I started counting quickly, and when my six-year-old brain skipped numbers, he'd tell me to start over and take my time. Reluctantly, I would start over and count slower, and finally, after what felt like an hour, I got to sixty. He smiled and we headed to the store.

What I Learned in Sixty Seconds

I often think about that afternoon with my dad because it helped inspire me and shape my perspective, especially in my financial life. My dad used something as simple as a single minute to teach me principles that have lasted decades, and he did it in such a practical way. Looking back, it is clear what I took away from that experience. I learned how long one minute was (which felt like forever at the time), how to count to sixty (by taking my time and focusing), and that each number between one and sixty mattered (skipping one single digit threw off the entire count and resulted in me having to start counting again from the beginning).

Fixing our personal finances can and - *should* take time. We're striving to make a transformational change, which helps redirect our financial path. So, we have to resist our own false sense of urgency, which pushes us to move so fast that we overlook important components and skip steps. Otherwise, we unintentionally leave gaps in the financial foundation we're seeking to build. When we inevitably go back to fix skipped steps, we end up spending more time than if we had just moved through our steps with intention. We must use care in our money journey so that we successfully go from one to sixty without unnecessary do-overs.

Each Step Is Essential

Simple steps are, by nature, less complex, and that can sometimes be a double-edged sword. Because of their simplicity, some people might mistakenly conclude that they are not as important as their more complex counterparts. And this can cause people to try to speed up the process by skipping to the steps they think are more important. What they don't see at the time is that the steps they've decided to skip are just as essential as the other steps, if not more so. Those steps tend to be the prerequisites to the next steps. If skipped, you risk having to repeat the entire process later or building a shaky foundation.

Remember Rachel in Chapter 3, "A Spoonful of Consistency and a Dash of Patience"? She created a rigid plan, skipped essential steps because she wanted the fast-track method, failed to accomplish her goals, and eventually found herself in that yo-yo cycle, repeatedly. This is precisely what happens when we skip steps.

If your plan used to have five big steps and now it has fifteen smaller steps, on the surface it might look like you're doing more. But, keep in mind, the new plan, although more steps, broke down all the big tasks and made them into smaller, bite-sized pieces that are much easier to accomplish. Now, each single step in your plan has a purpose, which means that step 8 is just as important as final step 15. If you skip one, you'll miss out on creating a sturdier foundation for your finances. Ultimately, every step matters, no matter how small it seems to be.

The Simplicity of Small Steps

At the core of our financial goals, simplicity will always win. Simplicity is more than just breaking big steps down into smaller ones. It also saves time, boosts our energy and confidence, and leads us to the finish line. With simple steps, you have more control, have more clarity, and see more progress. Simplicity is not a shortcut per se, but it does shorten the distance between you and your financial goals by clearly defining a road map that's easy to follow.

And once you start to experience small financial successes, you'll be motivated to continue, and over time you'll become more consistent in your steps. Each step you complete will help rebuild your habits and develop a lifestyle that supports your new financial journey. It's incredible what one small step can do in creating a positive ripple effect that takes you from financial stress to financial success.

As you plug forward in tiny increments, you exert less effort than you would with big tasks, so you won't need to frequently stop to rest or reset. And as you continue making progress, you build financial confidence that keeps you focused so you don't get distracted by other people's successes or timelines. Imagine reaching the same milestones as people who took the big leaps, but you took the easier route to get there. It's amazing when you can accomplish your goals without depleting all your mental energy in the process.

What Simplicity Can Do to Your Wealth

Let's look at the two new investors in Figure 5.1 and see how their steps mattered. Each investor is 25 years old and has the same goal: to retire at 55 years old. They both make $60,000 per year and want to retire as millionaires. Investor A decides to invest $5,000 once at the end of every year while investor B decides to invest $400 per month ($4,800 total per year). Both will invest in their preferred way for a total of 30 years. Before even starting the calculations, we can see that investor A will be investing $200 more per year than investor B, which indicates that A should be in the lead. But that's not the entire picture. Let's look further.

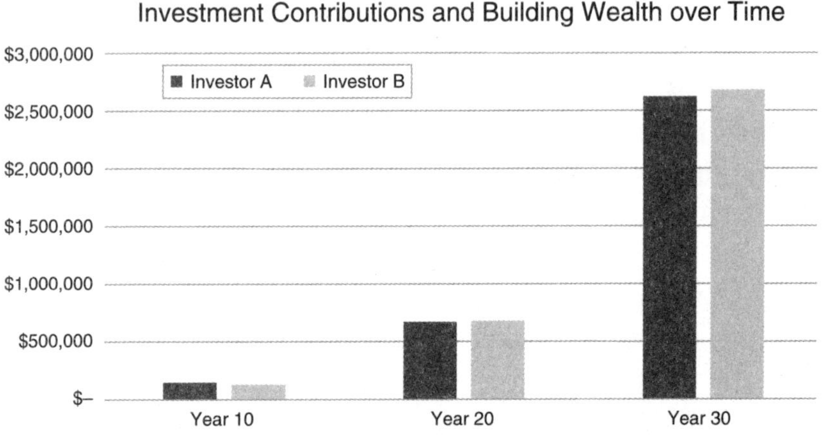

Figure 5.1

In the short term, investor A shows more investment growth than investor B. In the long term something magical happens. As we see in Figure 5.1, investor A was in the lead by about $18,000 more than investor B in year 10. In year 20, investor B catches up and takes the lead by about $3,500 more than investor A. And in year 30, investor B takes the lead again, by more than almost $57,000. Both investors cross the $2.5 million dollar threshold, even though one investor contributed less each year. That might seem odd at first glance. How could investor B take the lead and surpass investor A so substantially if their total investment was less by $6,000?

Investor B took advantage of compound interest by consistently contributing every month, which made compound interest work more in their favor. Compound interest is basically the interest you earn on top of interest. So let's say in month one, investor B contributed $400, and they received an average of 10% interest returns that month. They now have $440 going into month two, before contributions. So the next month, they would receive interest on their original $400 plus the $40 they earned, so they're earning interest on their interest earned! And that's just on that original $400—they will receive even more since they will continue to contribute an additional $400 every month. Compound interest is the ultimate wealth builder, and contributing early and consistently will help you take advantage of its power. In this case, simple steps unlocked more compound interest and, in turn, more wealth for investor B.

So far this is all great, but there's even more to this picture. Let's think beyond the math and interest and focus on their contribution amounts. If given the choice, which would you rather choose to contribute: $5,000 at the end of every year or $400 once per month? It's no secret that investor A has a much harder task of contributing $5,000, since A will need much more discipline to put that money aside throughout the year, and there is no real cadence to saving that money. A is essentially free to save it all in month one, save a little each month, or save it all at the very last minute before it's time to contribute. That freedom doesn't give enough structure to our plan, and when left to our own discretion, almost everything else will likely take priority. But when we have a monthly obligation, it's embedded in our spending plan and becomes a part of our day-to-day finances.

It's clear that investor B has a much easier task. By choosing a consistent contribution schedule, they automatically created a small-step plan to help them achieve their goal. B also eliminated some common barriers that tend to hinder people from saving consistently, which are heavy reliance on self-discipline and decision fatigue. Deciding on a smaller amount and including it in their monthly budget and spending plan automates the process and removes the stress of trying to figure out how and when to save the money. This results in a more consistent pattern of saving and contributing.

There is no doubt that both contribution plans have the potential to achieve a similar goal of becoming a millionaire at retirement. But if one plan eliminates barriers and makes saving easier, clearly that's the better option. The steps you choose to take matter when it comes to your consistency and overall success.

Choosing the Easier Way

As we've learned in previous chapters, when we choose big or complex tasks, they can be so intimidating that they cause us to procrastinate and delay doing them. In turn, we go into avoidance mode, not because we don't want to complete the task but because we feel the weight of it and immediately start making excuses for why we'll need more time, more energy, and more headspace to dedicate to this task. The result is that we don't start; we push it back to a later time and think someday we'll get to it, just not now. Then, to feel productive, we refocus our energy on an easier task because we know we can complete it.

Our brains prefer it when things are complete; it's why we love to know the end of a story, binge-watch television series, and hate cliff-hangers that don't close the loop. Because our brain prefers complete stories, we make the mistake of focusing on seemingly easy tasks, but they're only distractions from the tasks that move the needle. Instead, we should be focusing our tendencies and preferences on the small simple steps that investor B was taking.

Investor B chose what was realistic and doable for B and contributed consistently for 30 years, forming it into a habit that felt like second nature. Investors like B are able to enjoy their lives without worrying about their investments because their money is working for *them.*

Small Steps You Can Start Now

If you want to save money on your energy bill this month, some small steps might be unplugging small appliances after using them, turning your thermostat up or down a couple of degrees, turning off lights when you leave a room, purchasing a plug-in power saver, or joining an energy-saving program in your area or state. Whatever you decide to start with, understand that you don't have to have it all figured out right now. The important thing is to know what next step you are taking and focus on that. As you complete one step, then you can think of your next step. There's no sense in worrying about what's around the corner until you take the steps to get there first. Taking one step at a time creates a cadence that naturally integrates with your life so it works *with* it, not against it. It's much more effective to approach your finances this way.

Using Simple Steps for a Major Purchase

Let's look at another common scenario. Let's say you want to buy a new car. You might start by researching the type of car you want, figure out the price range you want to stay within, and find the make and model that works best for you. These steps are all a great start, and you might even feel ready to go to the dealership to start the negotiations and test-drive your new car, but are you fully ready?

While these are solid steps, there are other small steps that can help you even more. Let's better prepare our car-buying experience by saving money for the car, using what I like to call "set-and-get" funds. Set-and-get funds are savings accounts that are allocated for a specific purpose, in this case, your new car. Decide how much money you can save per month and automate the transfer from your bank or paycheck every month. Do this for a few months to test it out and ask yourself, Does it take too much from your income? Does it put a burden on your lifestyle? Are you getting annoyed when the money is transferred? Questions like these will provide insight on your purchase before you make the official commitment and give you the chance to change your mind before any obligations are made. Small steps like these can add a layer of mindfulness to your decision-making process and help you avoid impulsive, emotional spending decisions and more so, buyer's remorse.

So not only can small steps help you fix your finances, but they can also help you make more mindful decisions that affect your finances. Win-win.

We've already established that simple steps have the capability to completely transform your financial life, but impatience and the need for speed can sometimes overpower your decisions. So when you feel the urge to rush through a process, remember that skipping steps doesn't help you in the long run and tends to have an adverse effect. Instead, give each step it's time and attention so that you optimize your road to success, accomplish your goals, and avoid having to start back again from step one.

Chapter 6
The Simple Reboot

Every night after dinner, I like to clean my kitchen. I clear out the sink by placing all the dishes in the dishwasher as I wash the pots and pans by hand and lay them out to dry, and once I'm done, I complete the task with a good wipe down of the clean sink, countertops, and stove. After that, I take out tomorrow's meat from the freezer to thaw overnight in a bowl on the counter. As I look back at the kitchen just before I turn off the lights, I feel a sense of accomplishment and control over my space. This is part of what I like to call my "tidy stride," the cleaning routine that works for me.

Looking at my current routine, you'd think that I was a naturally organized and tidy person. But the truth is, I wasn't always this way. As I briefly explained in Chapter 1, "Big Goals Don't Budge," in the early part of my adulthood, I had developed an all-or-nothing mindset with any task I approached. I either cleaned everything or nothing at all. And almost always it was the latter. This mindset was compounded by the lack of chore expectations placed on me as a kid. When I was in grade school, my mom wanted me to focus only on my schoolwork, so I was not expected to clean or do any household chores other than occasionally helping with laundry and cleaning my room. Of course, there were bouts where I had the sudden urge to clean my room from top to bottom or completely empty my closet to reorganize, but cleaning was not a task I was expected to do regularly. My mom took care of almost all of it, and what teen would complain about the lack of cleaning responsibility? Certainly not me.

So when I became an adult and got married, my cleaning muscle was very weak. On many days, I did nothing, which resulted in spending most of my weekends tackling piles of dishes and messes for hours. During that time, I felt flustered, moody, and out of control, no doubt due to living in a constant state of disorder. Living that way doesn't exactly ease the mind, you know?

Establishing a Positive Routine

I don't remember exactly when things took a turn, but I remember the feeling that triggered the change. It was a Saturday, and I had just spent hours cleaning the entire house, top to bottom. I was happy that it was clean but also exhausted by all the work I had just done. My husband took care of the kids so that I could clean without distraction, and we were both completely out of energy. In that moment, an overwhelming feeling of frustration took over. I was sick and tired of the constant chaos in my space and in my mind. Sure, we were a young family with two small kids, so messy times were bound to occur, but I just knew that there must be a better system.

Since this was before the YouTube era, I had to find a better way by either asking people personally or figuring it out on my own. So I decided to think of some new methods to try on my own, first, and if that didn't work out, I'd go to plan B, which was to ask family and friends. After trying out a few methods, I found a simple routine that worked quite well and gave us back our weekends.

From Sunday to Thursday, I'd spend 20 minutes a day cleaning up one space in my home. Once the time was up, I stopped. This type of challenge motivated me to move quickly, and it became sort of like a game in my head. I had to finish the room I was cleaning before the clock ran out. And most days, I did, and it felt great! I'd also wash and dry one load of laundry per day and fold that load the next day along with my 20-minute cleanup time. By Thursday, the house was clean, laundry was washed and put away, and we had the weekend to relax.

Having a clean space also helped me stay in control of my finances. A clean kitchen encourages you to cook dinner at home more often instead of ordering takeout. A tidy living room invites more movie nights and entertaining friends and family rather than going out and paying for entertainment. Generally, when your space is clean, you're more likely to spend more time in it and spend less money because of it.

Recognizing When the System Needs to Change

My tidy stride worked well for years, until my season of life changed. My girls became teens and with all their activities outside of the home, our life became too busy to maintain our current routine.

It was time to make a change, but I knew that the framework of my system was solid and that some of the tasks still worked well, so I only needed to tweak a few things to make it work for me.

I decided that instead of completely creating a new system from scratch, I would reboot my current system. In the years that I used this routine, I had gained a lot of experience and knew how long each task took to complete, what tasks were essential for my day-to-day functions, and how much time I could reasonably spare to take care of those tasks.

Why a Reboot Is Better Than a Complete Redo

Just like rebooting a computer resets the applications and drives, a reboot in the context of this book takes the framework you've already created and resets the tasks, so they are more optimized. It allows you to change your routine without erasing everything you've accumulated in skills and experience. Just like with a computer, a simple reboot restarts the system, so it functions better when it starts back up. It doesn't perform a factory reset that wipes all the data clean; it just gives it a quick shutdown and restart so that it can get rid of any glitches and errors that slowed down or froze the processes.

That's exactly what I did to my cleaning routine, I did a quick reboot to use what worked and update what didn't so that my system was more optimized to serve my life. If I hadn't changed my cleaning habits, continuing to apply them to my new way of life would have eventually caused too many glitches and would have shut down my cleaning system altogether. We must recognize when it's time to adapt to our systems and when our systems need to adapt to *us*.

Rebooting the Reboot

When it came time to reboot my cleaning routine, I needed to determine which things needed to change. A reboot starts from where I am, so it makes it easier to keep the essential tasks while I reschedule or outsource those tasks that aren't as vital. My simple reboot looked like this:

- **Keep:** Most of kitchen cleanup, daily laundry, and meal planning and prepping.
- **Outsource to family:** Clean bedrooms, bathrooms, dining room, and living spaces.

And recently, I went through another reboot, basically rebooting my previous reboot. And it looks like this:

- **Keep:** Most of kitchen cleanup, laundry 2–3 times per week, and meal planning and prepping.
- **Outsource to professionals:** Deep clean of the entire house 1–2 times per month.

We do a light tidy clean once per week, but the full cleaning now goes to a professional cleaning service. Out of all the changes that were made with each reboot, some tasks remained the same throughout every season of my life. Those tasks were kitchen cleanup and meal planning and prepping. For me, these tasks are an essential part of my daily routine. When they are completed, I save money on groceries and eating out, which frees up money to use in other areas of my life such as saving and investing, updating parts of my home, saving for major purchases, or traveling with family and friends. And having the extra money allows us to have freedom of choice.

The Financial Reboot

Just as we applied a reboot to our home tasks, we've also applied several reboots to our financial life. On a macro level, our reboots looked like this:

- **Establishing a routine:** Budgeting, using cash envelopes, saving paper coupons, maintaining and updating grocery-saving systems, paying debt every month, and saving for emergencies.

- **First reboot:** Tweaking our existing routine, changing from paper coupons to digital coupons, and automating our savings.
- **Next reboot:** Again tweaking our most recent routine, automating our investments, and creating more income streams.

Of course, there are smaller tasks that we take care of as well, but these are major tasks that have helped us stabilize and create our financial security.

Your financial reboot will consider where you are, what you can handle right now, and what is needed for your finances to function at their best. It shouldn't be a cookie-cutter approach since we all have different circumstances, abilities, and priorities, and finding your balance may take an extra reboot or two. But, ultimately, rebooting allows you to keep what works, get rid of what doesn't, delete the completed tasks from your routine (such as "pay debt" once you're debt free), and optimize your steps based on your current season of life.

Understanding the 3A Framework

So how do you set up a reboot so that you can create a system that helps you fix your finances and still enjoy life at the same time? As I was working through my own reboots, I eventually created what I call the 3A framework to simplify the process. The 3As are Assess, Address, and Amplify. Each "A" covers one important step in the process of your reboot. Let's take a closer look at each one.

Assess

Review and evaluate your current routines, lifestyle priorities, and financial standing. In this step, you'll also determine what currently works well, what doesn't work at all, and what needs slight changes to work better for you. In this stage, you'll only analyze the information, so take your time in recognizing patterns, tendencies, and your day-to-day habits that resulted in where you are with your current finances.

It's crucial to keep in mind that this stage is solely to determine your starting point and where your strengths are; it's not to be used to make you feel guilt or shame because of your current situation or past mistakes you made.

Address

Start making changes. Based on your findings in the Assess step, start making the necessary changes to make progress in your finances. This is where the bulk of your effort will go. You'll create new tasks and slowly implement them in your daily routine, eventually creating new habits and routines in your daily life.

Amplify

Develop your new routines into systems that create accountability and keep you consistent. This is also where you'll track your progress and determine if the tasks are effective and efficient. You'll build systems that serve your financial goals while giving you the time freedom to live your life simultaneously.

Putting the 3A Framework into Action

In Chapter 4, "You've Done This Before, Now Do It with Intention," we talked about possible steps you could take to achieve the $10,000 emergency savings goal. While I didn't mention the

3A framework in that chapter, the steps we talked about there each fall into one of its stages! Let's match some of those steps to their appropriate stage.

- **Assess:** Check last month's bank statement, highlighting each expense type and adding up their totals (your current spending rate).
- **Address:** Create a budget that reflects your current spending rate. Add your new emergency savings fund to your savings section in your budget. Open a new savings account and name it "Emergencies." Distribute your salary among all your spending categories. Adjust your budget as needed so that your income minus expenses equals zero.

Although the example that we used in Chapter 4, "You've Done This Before, Now Do It with Intention," didn't apply the Amplify stage, it helped you get started and paved the way to go through the framework in order.

Now, let's dive a little deeper so you can see how to apply the entire 3A framework.

Goal 1: Budget Better

Here's how you could apply the 3A framework to improve your budget:

- **Assess:** Review the last three months of bank and credit card statements and determine your average spending total for each expense category (e.g., groceries, gas, shopping, eating out). We're reviewing three months to get an average spending rate. This helps us avoid any atypical months that might skew the numbers.

- **Address:** Create a new budget using the current spending totals from the Assess step. Adjust your spending so that your income covers all your expenses. Continue to research ways to save money in every area of your spending and reduce your category budgets where you can.
- **Amplify:** Automate your short-term and long-term savings. Use a tracker for your debt payments to keep yourself organized and more in control. Create a daily habit to spend five minutes per day reviewing your spending and budget to hold yourself accountable and remain consistent.

Goal 2: Pay Off Debt

You can also use the 3A framework to tackle debt:

- **Assess:** List all your debt (student loans, medical debt, credit cards, car loans, Buy-Now-Pay-Later loans; essentially everything except for mortgage) and add all your balances to get your grand total.
- **Address:** Pick a payoff method, such as the Debt Snowball method or the Debt Avalanche method. (I prefer the Avalanche method and explained how it worked in Chapter 2, "The Magic Power of Small Steps.") List your debt according to your method of choice, and then pay the minimum amount on every piece of debt while putting as much money toward the first item on the list until it is paid off. Repeat the process until you are debt free.
- **Amplify:** Periodically search for 0% APR promotional credit offers for balance transfers. Consolidate your debt by combining multiple balances to one card so you reduce the number of payments you make per month. Find ways to reduce

your spending so you have more money to pay toward debt. Create a side hustle to make extra money to pay even more debt faster.

The Flexibility of the 3A Framework

Again, each step leads you down the path of progress so you know exactly how to move forward with your goals without feeling overwhelmed or stuck. The 3A framework was designed to simplify the process and make it easy to apply to any financial goal you have.

Budgeting better and paying off debt are just two examples. You'll notice that this framework doesn't dictate what steps you must take but instead gives you a guideline of what to do first, next, and last, so you are consistently and confidently moving forward without confusion.

Each step in the framework plays a significant role that positively impacts your financial goals. The Assess step gives you clarity: you know where your starting point is and now have a better understanding of how to move forward. The Address step is all about action: you start implementing the plan so you can reach your new outcome. The Amplify step solidifies your steps: It helps you create systems to keep your new routines sustainable while providing a solid structure to ensure you stay on track and are consistently moving toward your goal. This step boosts your momentum and creates transformational change for your financial path.

Takeaways

Every habit you currently partake in affects your financial life one way or another, even if just slightly. Understanding this will provide valuable insight on how to reboot and reset your regular routines and systems so they support your financial goals in a much more impactful way. When you reboot your financial system, you're essentially rewiring some of the tasks without completely throwing away everything you have built and having to start from scratch. Starting from scratch is often more difficult than continuing where you stopped or got stuck. Continuing from your current step means you're already ahead, making it faster and easier to get back on track. It also gives you the opportunity to improve your current steps, modify them so they make sense with your lifestyle and priorities, and optimize your newly created systems so they continue pushing you toward achieving your financial goals. Rebooting is a soft reset for your habits, lifestyle, and eventually, your mindset, and it helps you improve without adding unnecessary pressure to start from zero and figure it out all over again. A financial reboot can be the difference between giving up and moving forward.

Chapter 7
No Such Thing as Too Basic

Have you ever heard the phrase "less is more"? This phrase is usually accompanied by a certain picture in my mind. The image is of a woman who isn't flashy or boastful in her appearance. She wears beautifully orchestrated ensembles, decorated with muted colors, but her clothing doesn't show logos or brand names. Her outfits are elevated with sprinkles of simple yet elegant jewelry, creating a grand statement, all while being completely understated. This is what I imagine to be the living definition of "less is more." Every piece of her outfit was executed well, creating a perfectly cohesive outward appearance.

On the surface, it might seem easy to be this basic, but the truth is that achieving this level of simplicity can be quite difficult. Committing to a basic style goes against everything that society promotes, so it requires us to have a mindset that values internal satisfaction rather than society's acceptance.

How Going Basic Benefits You

Adopting the "basic" standard has many benefits and offers a lot in terms of flexibility. Capsule wardrobes illustrate this flexibility easily. A capsule wardrobe takes a few basic pieces of clothing and creates dozens of outfit combinations that work well together, providing the person with the freedom to mix and match as much as they want. But for this clothing style to work well, it is key that the clothing pieces are basic enough to be interchangeable for mixing and matching. Going basic gives us the freedom to be flexible because it has less rules. It enables us to have an effortless routine and frees up more time that we can use to focus on more important things in our day.

The same can be said for your finances. When you take basic steps, you give yourself more freedom and flexibility. And there is no such thing as too basic, not in clothing, routines, or finances. Using simplicity in this way gives us the opportunity to remove some of the fluff and clean up our money routines. Creating a basic budget can help you clarify your priorities. Using a basic payment method for your debt helps you avoid getting stuck and keeps you moving forward. Implementing a basic grocery routine organizes your tasks and gives you a better way to control your grocery spending. Going the basic route strips out the complications and gives you easy, doable tasks to execute.

Understanding What Influences You

Unfortunately, going basic does not appeal to most people. As a society, many of us are influenced to buy more, have more, and want more. And most of our purchasing decisions are heavily influenced by what we see on social media. Our feed is filled with celebrities and influencers driving fancy cars, living in big, beautiful homes, and having bedroom-sized closets, which makes us want what they have. We buy into their seemingly perfect lifestyle, which looks exciting and fulfilling. Whether or not those influencers can afford their lifestyles is not what's relevant to us in the moment. All we see is a life of luxury, and we are convinced we need it.

It is important to look at the entire picture, not just the small highlights that we see. Most influencers fall into one of three categories. A select few are truly wealthy and can afford the lifestyle they show on their pages. Some of them receive most of their products for free and are paid to promote certain items and brands. And many of them are drowning in debt but don't share this detail openly. And since we only see a bit of their highlight reel, we're intrigued and want to have what they have.

I know exactly how this feels and what it does to your mindset because years ago it influenced my spending decisions too. It caused us to live paycheck-to-paycheck, in debt, and constantly stressed. Now that we're debt free, I've become more careful with how I spend money. And that helped me notice how incredibly easy it is to slip into extreme consumerism without realizing it. An expensive shopping habit can form without much effort if we're not careful. And before we know it, we can find ourselves in more debt and less control.

According to an article from debt.org, consumer debt in the United States continues to climb every year. Refer to Table 7.1 for the average amount of debt by generation in the year 2020.

Do these numbers surprise you? The sad truth is that as consumerism grows, so does debt. The more we buy, the more we rely on debt to pay for it. And in our current world, we tend to always want more, even if it means making payments for years to cover the cost.

Sadly, our current shopping habits almost never lead to happiness. Sure, you get a temporary dopamine hit that makes you feel happy in the moment, but when that wears off, you're left with more things to maintain and more of your hard-earned money

Table 7.1 Generational Debt in the Year 2020

Generation	Age Range	Average Debt
Gen Z	18 to 23	$16,043
Millennials	24 to 39	$87,488
Gen X	40 to 55	$140,643
Baby boomers	56 to 74	$97,290
Silent generation	75 and above	$41,281

wasted on paying debt and interest. And what's worse is that it seems to create a cycle: The more that we buy and accumulate, the more we seem to want. Our eyes become bigger than our wallets can handle. It reminds me of an Arabic saying: "Ma yimlash aeyno gher el torab," which loosely translates to "The only thing that fills one's eyes is dust." Basically, it can be interpreted to mean that greed is a part of human nature. One is often never fully satisfied with anything one has, always wanting and seeking more. Greed can cause a lot of harm to your finances if you're not careful.

The Health of Your Finances Starts with Your Happiness

Since material things do not have enough power to fill an internal void or provide happiness, then we need to redefine what it means to be happy. One simple way to figure it out is the deathbed scenario. If you were on your deathbed, what things would you wish you had more of? For some, it might be more time with family, traveling and seeing beautiful sights, a deeper relationship with God, or having the freedom to do anything. All those wishes share one common trait, which is they don't require anything material. They don't require an extra big closet, a fancy car, or a seven-bedroom McMansion. So why do we have to wait until we're on our deathbed to realize what is important to us? I'm willing to bet if you thought about it right now, you could come up with a list of nonmaterial things that make you feel fulfilled. And nothing on your list would be based on an ad you saw or a social media post on your feed.

For all these reasons, it is time to get back to basics. Refocus your attention on what is important to you at the core, and in turn, you will be able to simplify your finances, so it reflects only your new priorities. Since your finances should always be a direct reflection of your lifestyle and priorities, simplifying your goals will automatically simplify how you spend and where you direct your money. Trimming your finances down to the basics is not meant to restrict or deprive you; rather, it is meant to provide clarity, better organization for your money, and more focus on the things that matter most to you. As a result, it will naturally remove the expenses that no longer fit your new lifestyle so that you have more money for the things that matter the most to you.

How Basics Transformed My Finances

I found the basics to be a game changer for my finances. When I wanted to save money on groceries, I first looked at my pantry. I literally walked to the kitchen, opened my pantry, and wrote a list of items I had on hand. Then, I went online and found a few websites that would generate recipes from ingredients I typed in. The websites provided meal combinations that were creative, used what I had, and ultimately saved me money. With just these two basic steps, I was able to make at least one or two pantry meals to feed my family each week. Every meal we made at home helped us avoid takeout, which saved us about $50 a week at the time. That, in addition to spending less on groceries for the week, meant that we were saving about $75 just from two extremely simple steps. I feel the need to mention that these steps didn't take me more than 5–10 minutes to complete on a weekend. So I spent about 10 minutes per week to save $75. That's how the basic plan works.

This is how I was able to transform my finances, small step by small step. After just those two basic steps, I was excited to add more steps to my routine to help me save even more money for the week. So I added stockpiling. The goal of stockpiling is to stock up on the items you use regularly and the items that are shelf-stable, meaning they can last a long time without refrigeration. I already knew a little about stockpiling because my mom was a pro at storing enough essentials to last us a few months. Starting out, I kept my stockpile list basic, too. I decided to stock up on flour, sugar, rice, pasta, tea, and some canned goods such as tomato puree and beans. These six or seven items helped me make countless different meals for my family. While I can't remember how much money this helped me save at first, I will say that it completely transformed the way I shop for groceries, even to this day. This one step helped me realize that I could take better advantage of sale prices and save a lot more money on the cost of each item.

The great thing about the concept of basics is that you can't do it wrong. The simpler you make your steps, the better. There is no such thing as making it too basic. If the step feels too easy, that's a good thing! It means that you've found steps that work well with your lifestyle; steps that make it easy to move forward and make progress are naturally going to be more sustainable with your lifestyle. As you create and apply basic steps, you essentially foolproof your routines to make more progress and achieve your financial goals with clarity and ease. And knowing that you can't mess it up gives you more confidence, so you're motivated to do even more.

Simplifying your finances and going back to basics filters out the things that don't provide happiness and gives you room to add in the things that do. It also gives you the freedom to create and set up a financial path that works for you based on what matters most.

Are You the Fisherman or the Businessman?

We all have different priorities and because of that, the path we choose will be unique to us. When I think of financial paths, I'm reminded of a story I heard in a church sermon one Sunday. It was a story written by Paulo Coelho called "The Fisherman and the Businessman."

The story talks about this fisherman, who lives a basic life in a small village near the water. His daily routine consists of fishing in the morning, playing with his kids, taking a nap with his wife, and spending time with friends over a few drinks in the evening. A businessman notices him fishing and suggests some steps the man can take to make him more successful. He goes on to say that the fisherman should spend more time fishing, so he can earn more money to buy a bigger boat, catch more fish, get more money to buy more boats, eventually open a distribution center and become rich. At each stage of the businessman's plan, the fisherman asks him what's next. By the end, the businessman says that the fisherman will finally be able to retire, move to a nice place near the water, fish in the morning, play with his kids, nap with his wife, and spend time with his friends. The fisherman replied, "Isn't that what I'm doing now?"

I chuckled the first time I heard this story, but the truth is, this story perfectly illustrates what many of us do with our finances. Sometimes, we make things harder than they need to be because we're convinced the hard way is *the only* way to success. The good news is, most of the things we want are easier to reach than we think; we just need to change the road map to achieve them. If our road map has more basic, clear steps, then we'll have an easier time getting to our financial goals. Creating an easier path isn't about taking shortcuts; it's about being strategic with your time by simplifying the path and creating less resistance on your journey. As a result, you're able to build momentum and make more progress with your finances. So be clear about your goals, and create a road map that shortens the distance it takes to reach your financial goals.

Part III

Grocery Savings

Chapter 8
From Spendthrift to Savvy Shopper

If you don't know how to manage a dollar, you won't know how to manage ten. This is not only the philosophy I use to manage my finances in general, but it's also one that has helped me substantially with my grocery budget. It's quite easy to spend more on groceries than you anticipate, mainly because it's a commodity we all have to buy in order to survive. Since it's an essential part of our life, it's easy to justify paying more or overlooking prices when we add items to our cart.

Years ago, I didn't know what a grocery budget was. You might think I'm joking, but I'm being serious. We're not formally taught how to purchase groceries, perhaps because it seems like it would be self-explanatory. You need food, you go to the store, you buy food, mission accomplished. But there is a lot more that goes into shopping for groceries than just deciding that you need something and putting it in your cart. The decisions you make impact your finances and those micro-decisions eventually translate to spending more on groceries than you need to.

Growing up, my mom did all the grocery shopping. I went with her sometimes, pushed the cart, and helped her bring the groceries in from the car, but that was the extent of my involvement with this task. But when I got married and had to shop for my own family's groceries, I didn't really have a method to my shopping routine. I just haphazardly shopped when we ran out of something, when I was craving something, or when I needed ingredients for a recipe I wanted to make. That's not exactly a formula for saving money. Who knew I needed a money-saving formula for grocery shopping? I certainly didn't.

At the time, I didn't realize that how I shopped for groceries could have such a big impact on my finances. It might sound like an exaggeration, but the reality is that your grocery budget affects every other area of your finances. In fact, every area of your finances directly or indirectly affects the other areas, no matter how big or small that area may seem.

Beginning to Budget

When I first started shopping for groceries for my young family of four, I would go to the closest grocery store, get whatever looked good without checking the price, pay with a credit card, and walk out. My shopping routine didn't include a budget, and that made it difficult to recognize when I was overspending since I didn't set a spending limit. Not having a budget also meant that I could buy anything I wanted, which resulted in me becoming a spendthrift, not only in the area of groceries but in most areas of my spending. My shopping habits made it difficult to have extra money to use in other areas of our finances, such as paying off debt or saving money for emergencies.

For many years, I thought that we just needed to *make* more money to cover our monthly spending. It took me a while to realize that it wasn't an income problem; it was a spending problem. I needed to manage my money better. As you can probably imagine, this was during my budget-hating era, before I learned how helpful a budget can be. Since groceries *are* a necessity, I didn't think it made sense to enforce a spending limit. But without a grocery budget, I didn't really know how much I could *afford* to spend on food per month. And if I didn't understand what we could reasonably afford, how could I expect my income to just magically be enough?

I had no idea how much financial damage my mindset caused at the time, but the truth is, it was one of the main reasons behind our struggle with money. It directly influenced my spending behavior, and because of that, we lived paycheck-to-paycheck and were always one paycheck away from financial disaster. It wasn't until we were buying our first house that I finally took budgeting seriously and became an active partner in managing our money. According to my husband, it was the only way we'd be able to fully take control of our finances. That's when we accounted for our very first grocery budget.

My original budget was based on what we had spent the month before. So our budget was set at $1,200 per month. Sometimes, I'd go over budget and spend about $1,500 per month, but for the most part, I spent within this range.

This initial budget, as we'll learn in Chapter 9, "Get More and Pay Less," was still incredibly high. But, at least at this point, I had a limit to work within. That limit forced me to think a little more about my purchases, at least in reducing the frequency of my impulsive cart adds.

To be honest, I didn't think this was going to substantially improve our financial situation. But it was the small step I needed to get the ball rolling in the right direction. Setting a dollar limit really started to shift the way I thought about my grocery spending. And even though most of my shopping habits hadn't changed yet, I started keeping a mental shopping list and began to slowly change the type of foods I bought to stay on budget.

Using Cash Envelopes Is a Game Changer

Since I had a tendency to overspend, I wanted to find something that would help me save more and spend less, so I started using cash envelopes. Cash envelopes are a great way to take control of a challenging spending area in your budget. Using a cash envelope instead of a credit or bank card helps you take better control. Here are some of the benefits I found when I used a cash envelope.

1. It gives you a hard cash limit, and once the money is gone, it's gone. So you are much more careful with how you spend your budget.
2. Since it is generally more painful to pay with cash than with a plastic card, you naturally think about your purchase before making the decision to pay for it.
3. Using cash also minimizes the number of items mindlessly added to your cart, since you'll need to make sure you have enough to cover the cost when you pay the cashier. Otherwise, you may have to request that the cashier void an item or two, often in front of a line of other shoppers, which—trust me—is not a great experience.

Using cash envelopes is a pretty simple process, but it can take a little time to adapt to the boundaries it creates for you. However, this spending tool makes you look at your spending habits in a different way. I gradually became more intentional with the items I was putting in my cart, comparing similar items to see what was cheaper, and questioning whether the item I added was necessary or if I could use another ingredient I already had at home.

After a few months of practice, I learned how to pace my spending. It took a little while to get used to using cash, and at first, I spent most of my cash budget during the first two weeks of my shopping. Then, I'd struggle to get everything we needed for the last two weeks. So I decided to separate my budget into weekly limits to help me balance out my spending. Eventually,

I found my stride and was able to stretch the money across the entire month.

Choosing Private Label Brands

Private label brands are usually the store brands of your favorite items. They are generally located on the same shelf next to the national brand of the same item. Oftentimes, private labels cost less than national labels. Your savings can add up substantially if you choose to buy private labels instead of national brands.

Although you can clearly see the price difference, many people think that private label varieties just don't taste good or that there must be something mediocre about them if they cost less than the national brand. But in most cases, that's completely inaccurate. Surprisingly, many of the private label and national brand foods are manufactured in the same factory, using the exact same ingredient list. If you don't believe me, feel free to check the labels and compare the list of ingredients on your favorite item next time you visit a grocery store. With that understood, private labels might be more appealing since you aren't sacrificing flavor or quality by paying the lesser price. And you're able to save more money each time you swap out a national brand with a private label (if there isn't a special sale or coupon that makes the national brand cheaper that week) with each shopping trip.

When I first tried this swap, I was shocked to see such a difference in my spending because of such a small change. Most of the time, I was able to save $100 to $150 each month with this method, and that made it much easier for me to stay within my budget while still being able to purchase the items we needed.

Taking Advantage of Store Coupons and Weekly Deals

When I was still fairly new to grocery shopping, I decided to learn a few more methods that could help me stay on budget and save money. One of the easiest methods I found was using store coupons that were located in the weekly ads. To be clear, I wasn't checking my ads every week, but when I visited the store, I'd pick up an ad as I walked in and browse quickly to see if they had coupons I could use.

Store coupons along with other store incentive deals such as buy X items for Y dollars, buy one get one free (BOGO), or mix-and-match options helped me stock up on some items and save money at the same time.

Turning Saving into a Sustainable Practice

I continued using these strategies and making minor improvements along the way until I finally felt in control of my spending. I went from overspending every month to creating a basic system that helped me stick to my $1,200 budget without feeling deprived. At the time, $1,200 was still higher than necessary for a family of four in my region. But the goal at first wasn't to drastically change my budget; it was to take one small step in creating and sticking to that budget. As we talked about in Chapter 6, "The Simple Reboot," it's important that you take small steps, assess where you are in the process, and work with where you are to gradually make progress toward where you want to be.

I was not in a place to cut back just yet. I needed to first stabilize my spending before learning how to reduce my budget. In Chapter 9, "Get More and Pay Less," we'll talk more about how I went from spending $1,200 per month to just $400 per month and how I am still able to stick to my $400–$450 budget, even now. (Yes, really!)

But for all intents and purposes, I think it's important to share that going from spendthrift to savvy shopper is a process that is meant to be a gradual progression, not a drastic one. Remember gradual is sustainable, drastic is not, so starting with very small steps was key to keep me moving forward without overwhelming me. And using this approach worked well; I was able to accomplish the following:

- Create a grocery budget based on what I usually spent.
- Find easy ways to save money so I didn't overspend.
- Learn how to take better control of my impulse purchases.
- Stay consistent.

With these small changes that I made in the span of several months, I saw a noticeable shift in my mindset and spending behavior. Eventually, I went from being a mindless spendthrift who lived paycheck-to-paycheck to becoming a savvier shopper and spender who took time to think about her purchases. This mindfulness created abundance in our budget, we were no longer overspending, at least in this area, and it gave us a little more breathing room. This milestone eventually started a financial shift that would prompt us to pay off all our debt, save a six-month emergency fund, and start investing for retirement. While I don't use cash envelopes anymore, the structure and discipline it instilled in me still influences how I manage my spending to this day.

If you told me back then that managing my grocery spending and saving money would afford me a life I loved, I wouldn't have believed you. Before making these changes, I didn't have an accurate understanding of how each area of our finances played a significant role in our overall financial health. During that season of my life, my age group seemingly spent money as if it were free, and no one else seemed to pay much attention to their grocery budget. So, deciding to create a plan for my groceries and reaching a milestone of taking control of my grocery spending was quite an accomplishment for me. Sometimes it still shocks me how something as simple as grocery shopping could make such a drastic impact.

Becoming Savvier

Savviness comes in stages. Start small and build on what you learn by adjusting and adding to your strategy. As you save more money and become more confident, you'll explore newer methods that you can try. As time goes on, you'll find a routine that works well for your lifestyle, and it will become a system you rely on to buy the things you want without paying full price.

Savvy Spending Means Savvy Saving

It's no mystery that when you shop smarter, you'll spend less and save more. It's important to point out that our goal isn't to just save more money. No, saving money helps us accomplish our bigger goals, such as becoming debt free, being financially independent, and building wealth and financial security. Saving money gives us the means to reach our goals.

Saving money for the sake of saving has no true purpose. We're not on this earth to collect paper; we're here to live full, enjoyable, and stress-free lives. The money you save becomes a tool to enable you to live a life you want. And to think that you can accomplish all that you want by first starting with something as small as your grocery budget—now that's the magic of small steps.

Chapter 9
Get More and Pay Less

"It's still cheaper than takeout. I'm saving money," I would tell myself as I freely grabbed expensive ingredients off the shelves and filled my cart without rhyme or reason. Once I would get home, I'd diligently put everything away, having the best of intentions to cook every day and feed my family better.

While I did find myself cooking more at home and eating less takeout overall, I didn't see much savings, and our budget totals didn't change much. What I wasn't spending on takeout food I was spending at the grocery store. On average, I spent $1,200 to $1,500 per month on groceries for our family of four. This was around 2008, and at the time my kids were both under the age of seven and weren't big eaters. Spending that much on groceries *might* have been justified if I used up everything I bought. But, sadly, a lot of our groceries would go to waste because I wouldn't get to them fast enough.

Whether you think this total is a lot or not enough, the point is that my grocery game was severely lacking. We were still living paycheck-to-paycheck, but now we weren't even enjoying the occasional fast-food takeout. I was frustrated because I didn't know how to fix this.

Know What a Tomato Is Really Worth

One day, I was shopping for groceries while I was on the phone with my mom. As usual, I would share how much items cost as I shopped because she loved keeping up with grocery prices and was great at spotting a good deal. In that moment, I picked up some tomatoes to put in the cart; she asked how much they were, and I answered, "Three ninety-nine per pound." I remember this vividly because her response completely changed my perspective on grocery shopping. My mom told me that I should never pay that much for tomatoes, and then she named a few stores near me that sold tomatoes for seventy-nine cents per pound.

I was shocked at the price difference. Surely, there must be something wrong with those cheaper tomatoes, I thought. But I decided to put back my items anyway and head to one of the stores my mom mentioned. It was the wildest thing! Not only did they have tomatoes for seventy-nine cents per pound, but all their produce was also a fraction of the cost of the other grocery store! I suddenly realized that my previous thoughts of justifying spending more at the grocery store—by reminding myself that the items cost less than takeout—were flawed. Just because my groceries cost less than a restaurant meal didn't mean I was saving money. I needed to be more mindful of the prices and what I was choosing to purchase.

Learning and Changing

As a newbie who severely lacked grocery shopping skills, my produce-shopping experience opened the door to so many questions. I was thrilled to start learning how my mom saved money on her groceries, so I started asking her about her grocery budget, how much she typically spent, how much I should reasonably spend for my family size, and so on.

What I found out was that her grocery budget as an empty nester was about $100 per month, and many months she even came in under budget. For my family size, she suggested starting at $300, since my kids were still young and didn't eat very much. At first, that sounded impossible to me, but as I developed the shopping skills that I discuss in this chapter, I was surprised at what I could do with my budget.

My mom also taught me the importance of planning ahead, checking my weekly ads, stocking up on staple ingredients when they were on sale, cooking dinners that would use up all that I purchased, and understanding that my grocery savings always starts at home, not in the store.

With her help, I started making a few changes that helped me save money that first week. I started checking my ads, and because I was still learning my prices, I would call my mom to confirm which items were actually good deals. I started writing a shopping list because I had mom-brain and would often forget what I needed but also because I could organize my list based on the sale items so I didn't miss out on potential savings. Then, I slowly started to stock up on staple ingredients, items such as rice and pasta, potatoes, beans, canned tomato puree, oil, and flour. These items are shelf-stable and can last a long time, so stocking up on them meant I always had them on hand and I wouldn't run the risk of wasting them if I didn't get to them in a few days.

My Grocery Coach

My mom became my grocery shopping coach, my go-to person to ask "on the spot" questions when I was in the store and wasn't sure if I should buy something. With her help, I started developing my grocery shopping skills and started seeing my hard work pay off in terms of savings. I started applying more strategies, some from my mom and others that I read or heard about and found what worked and what didn't for my lifestyle.

After a few months, I had created a basic grocery routine that helped me save money every week without much effort. My new routine worked *with* my lifestyle, which made it easy to maintain. It helped me get the items my family needed, save money, and enabled me to make meals my family and I loved.

Since then, my grocery routine has evolved and had several iterations. Once I mastered my grocery game, I was able to get my budget down to just $250 per month. Then, as my kids grew a little older, I increased my budget to $300 per month. And currently, we spend between $400 and $450 a month.

I say all this to show you that transforming your grocery budget and creating a routine that works for you takes time. And that's the beauty of a slow and steady transformation. It enables you to get used to your new routine, swap out steps that don't work for your lifestyle, and create a routine and system that grows your savings step by step. And once you create a solid routine that works, you'll be able to buy more of the foods you need and want and pay less for them.

How to Create a Routine That Saves Money

To save money on your groceries, you need to plan the steps you'll take each week to help you prepare for a successful shopping trip. If I were starting again today, I would do this:

Step 0: Determine Your Grocery Budget

This step isn't done every week, but it's important that you start here so you can create a reasonable game plan for your budget.

Typically, a good rule of thumb is to aim for about $100 per person, per month. Let's talk a little about what this budget covers and doesn't cover.

- It covers food for everyone in your household, including young children and babies.
- It doesn't cover paper goods, toiletries, or cleaning supplies. Add a separate line item in your budget for these items. I usually add $50 to $100 per month, and I tend to buy enough to last about two or three months. Test out your budget amount to see what amount works best for you.

It's also important to note that this amount is an average, so you may find that your true budget is a little higher or lower than $100 per person per month, depending on your region, the stores near you, the availability of products, and so on. This dollar amount is meant to be a starting point, not a hard-and-fast rule that you must abide by. Start with this budget, and then adjust as you need to.

Step 1: Check Your Local Sales Ads

Up to this very day, I still check my local ads for weekly sales. This is where you get all your intel before ever stepping foot in the grocery store. Your ads don't just tell you what's on sale. They also enable you to compare prices across all your local stores so you know which market to visit this week. Stores *should* be in competition for your business, and this is the way to make sure that you are always paying the lowest prices.

If you don't get your weekly ads sent to you, don't worry: there is an app that can show you the same information, called the Flipp app. I love this app because it not only shows you the sales and helps you compare prices between stores, but it also allows you to search for the items you need so you can see exactly where to get them at their lowest price.

Step 2: Compare Unit Prices Across Stores

If you're like me when I first started, then you might not know how to properly compare prices (yes, there is a right and wrong way to do it). The most important number you need to pay attention to is not the total price of the item but the unit price.

The unit price gives you the price per unit, and a unit can be an ounce, pound, each, bag, package, and so on. To know your unit price, divide the total amount for your unit total by the number of units. And now stores have made it even simpler for you to see your unit prices. They usually have them printed on the shelf sticker; it's usually printed in a small font and located either under or to the side of the total price.

Unit prices do more than just help you figure out which grocery stores have the best prices; they also help you compare prices between grocery stores and warehouse stores. And for the record, warehouse stores don't always have the best prices; that's why it's so important to compare unit prices so you know if you're getting the best deal.

For example, let's say that a box of 30 individual potato chip bags costs $12; then the unit price is $12/30 bags = $0.40 per bag, which is essentially per serving.

Let's compare it to a family-sized bag that also has 30 servings (to keep things simple), and assume the bag costs $7. The unit price would be $7/30 = $0.23 per serving.

Looking at unit price, we can be 100 percent sure that the family-sized bag costs less and gives the same amount in servings.

You'll be shocked with how much money you can save just with this step alone!

You can start keeping track of your unit prices with what I like to call a grocery price list, which we'll look at next.

Step 3: Compare Sale Prices to Your Grocery Price List

Your grocery price list is basically a list of your regularly purchased items so you can keep track of the prices and know when to stock up. Figure 9.1 shows the grocery price list that my coaching community, Super Savers uses, as an example.

GROCERY PRICE LIST (DAIRY)

DATE	ITEM	BRAND	TOTAL PRICE	UNIT PRICE	NOTES

Figure 9.1

Your grocery price list helps you do these things:

- **Determine if a sale price is truly a good deal.** Not everything on sale is actually a good deal. If tomatoes are on sale this week for $2 per pound, and I compare it to my price list where I paid $1.50 per pound for tomatoes last week, then it's easier to determine that $2 per pound isn't a great sale price, and I can then look at other stores to get a better price.
- **Know when to stock up on an item and save money.** If your grocery price list shows that you paid $2.50 for a loaf of bread and it's currently on sale for $1 each, then you can buy five and freeze them for a month or two until the next major sale.
- **Become aware of subtle price increases over time so you can make necessary adjustments to your budget.** Grocery prices increase subtly (and sometimes not so subtly) over time. It's important to recognize when this is happening so you can gradually increase your grocery budget to adapt to new, permanent price increases.
- **Know which stores are budget-friendly and offer the best prices in your area.** Savvy shoppers know which stores are the best at saving the most money, and the grocery price list helps you become a savvy shopper.

Using a grocery price list is fairly simple. After each shopping trip, sit down with your grocery price list (in paper or digital form) and your shopping receipt. Record the items and prices you paid based on the receipt, as well as the quantity and unit price (as previously explained, to get the unit price, take the total price and divide by the number of units for that item. For example, 10 packs of chips for $10 would be $1 per unit).

You'll need to update your grocery price list from time to time, but many of the items will have a pretty consistent price from week to week. Maintaining your list is definitely worth the effort.

Step 4: Write Your Shopping List

Many people still go to the grocery store with a mental list. And often, they end up forgetting at least one item only to discover that they've forgotten it when they need it most. Most of us lead busy lives, and we just don't have enough mental capacity to maintain a grocery list on top of everything else we need to remember. Keeping a mental list is often a recipe for failure.

To avoid this, make sure to write a shopping list before you head to the store. But we're not going to just stop there. It's not just about writing any old list; your list needs to save you money, so the way you write your list matters.

Before you write your list, you need to do the following:

- Check your ads (as we mentioned previously in step 1).
- Shop your pantry, freezer, and fridge first to make sure you use up what you've already paid for.
- Create a menu plan based on what is on sale that week in combination with what you already have on hand. This essentially leaves only some remaining supplemental items that you'll pick up this week from the store.

Now, you're ready to write your shopping list, a list that not only uses what you already have but takes advantage of the current sales and saves you money this week and every week.

Step 5: Stock Up on Sales

One of the easiest ways to save money and have everything you need on hand is to stock up on your groceries when they are on sale. And now that you know how to use your weekly ads and grocery price list to determine which prices are the lowest, you'll know which items to stock up on each week.

Stocking up when prices are at their lowest means you never have to pay full price again, and that's a wonderful thing! A good rule of thumb is to stock up for six to eight weeks at a time, which is typically the sales cycles for most items, so that's when that item will likely go back on sale.

Step 6: Learn How to Meal Plan

Meal planning plays a major role in helping you create a better shopping experience. And if done well, it not only helps you save money, but it can help you save time as well. My favorite meal plan options enable me to keep things simple but feed my family the meals they love.

Here are a couple of meal options that you can include in your meal plan to help you get started.

Takeout Fake-Out

This is probably one of our favorites. This type of meal does two things: It helps you get a meal on the table that you know your family will enjoy, and it helps satisfy your takeout cravings without the added expense.

Takeout fake-out recreates your favorite takeout meals at home. The bonus is that you get to add or take away any of the ingredients, so the meal is made just the way you like it. You also get the added benefit of knowing exactly what went into your dish, so there won't be any unnecessary additives or preservatives. And perhaps my favorite benefit is that it saves a lot of money without sacrificing flavor.

Leftover Makeover

It's exactly as the name suggests, and this is great for those of you who either don't like leftovers or who have family members who don't like leftovers. Leftover makeovers take leftovers and transform them into a completely new dish. For example, pot roast that turns into tacos or burrito bowls the next day or leftover baked chicken that turns into chicken and broccoli casserole. It's a simple way to use up what you already have and save time in the kitchen. And when you know in advance that certain meals are likely to turn in leftover makeovers as you make your shopping list, you can reduce the number of groceries you need to buy to cover all your meals. It's a win-win.

Pennies Become Dollars

Applying these steps and strategies can help you generate a lot of savings each week. They are my favorite methods to use because they work well and they don't take up a lot of your time. These methods helped me take my grocery budget from $1,200 (at its lowest) to about $400 per month, which is a 66 percent savings on my groceries. Let's take a quick look at how all of these things fit together, along with a couple of lessons from Chapter 8, "From Spendthrift to Savvy Shopper":

- Determine your grocery budget.
- Create a grocery price list with unit prices included, and use it to compare sales prices and get the best deals.
- Write your shopping list down. Don't try to memorize it.
- Check your pantry, freezer, and fridge so you don't buy items you don't need.
- Use cash envelopes to help you curb your spending and stick to your budget.
- Choose private-label brands over national brands.
- Take advantage of store coupons, weekly ads, and other sales.
- Create meal plans based on what you have and what's on sale.
- Reduce your takeout spending by recreating some of those meals with takeout fake-out.
- Plan leftover makeovers into your shopping list so you can eat more meals from fewer purchases.
- Stock up in advance when prices are good on shelf-stable items.

Each of these methods are helpful and even more impactful when they're used together. For example, let's say you want to create a takeout fake-out meal this week. Your grocery price list gives you the cost of each ingredient for that meal, so you can see how much you save by cooking at home instead of buying that takeout meal. The price list also gives you a basis to easily compare previous prices to this week's sales ads to see if it's worth stocking up on those items to use for another time. And if you have leftovers from your takeout fake-out meal, you can repurpose it by creating a leftover makeover. Each step saves money. And your savings quickly compound on each other like interest.

On the surface, grocery savings might seem too small to make a difference with your finances. In my experience, grocery savings are the perfect gateway to get you started. And once you see your savings multiply, you'll soon realize how much of an impact it can make on your financial transformation. Remember, the small steps you take now push you to conquer financial milestones down the road.

Chapter 10
Creating a Savings Ecosystem

Saving money for a month or two is fairly easy. You can drastically cut your spending in the short term by restricting your lifestyle to only eating at home, finding free entertainment, and pinching every penny until it screams. This is one approach that can help you save a lot of money quickly. But if you want to consistently save money every single month *without* severely depriving yourself of your beloved lifestyle, then you need a more thoughtful and strategic plan, one that you can implement easily but gradually so that it takes shape and molds to your lifestyle preferences and priorities.

Implementing this type of change may take a bit longer, but once you refine what works for you, you'll begin to notice how it transforms your budget. Your mindfulness will help you spend less, and your savings will visibly start to grow to exciting totals.

So far, the steps we've discussed in previous chapters to help you with your grocery savings will help stabilize your budget and move you forward in a steady pace. But what if I told you that what you've learned so far is only part of the equation to saving money? In this chapter, we'll explore the other side of that equation and focus our attention on our home systems and routines, specifically how we run our kitchen duties.

Setting Your Kitchen Up for Success

Perhaps one of the most important things to keep in mind is that saving money on groceries always starts at home first, not in the store. What we do in the store is directly affected by our preparation beforehand. Our kitchen is the heart of our system, and it needs to run as efficiently as a money-making grocery store. Our goal is to organize our kitchen in such a way that we know what we have on hand, what we need to buy more of, and how much we need to buy.

This combination is what sets us up to save massively every week. When we know everything about our food stock, we're able to make better choices on what to stock up on and when, and that creates a shopping cycle that coincides with sales on those items.

For example, let's say I have an organized freezer that has a separate section for ground beef, stew meat, chicken breast, shrimp, and fish. I organize each section in the "first in, first out" (or FIFO) method, a well-known method of stock rotation used by grocery stores to ensure that they always sell the oldest items first and stock the newest items in the back of the shelf. I pay attention to how much I have of each item in stock. When I'm down to about three weeks of ground beef left, I have enough time to search for sales and compare prices so that I can get more ground beef at the lowest price possible. Because I've been using my grocery price list, which keeps track of the unit price I paid for each item, it's easy for me to make sure I'm paying a good price. Since I have a three-week supply, I'm not in a rush to buy immediately, which gives me time to check all my options before stocking up.

This is one way that your organized freezer will help you save money, but there is another method that works just as well. This is the one I typically use, and it doesn't require me to check my stock because the sales dictate how often I buy my items.

Let's use the same example of stocking up on ground beef. Instead of checking my stock, I'll check the weekly sales ads to find out when ground beef is on sale, at which point I will stock up with enough supply to last six to eight weeks at a time. What's the significance of stocking up for six to eight weeks at a time? Well, that's a standard sale cycle for most grocery items. So if you follow this method, every six weeks or so, you will stock up, and you'll never run out of that item or ever need to pay full price. Every food item you use has a sale cycle. As you work on your kitchen system, you will take notice of these cycles, which will help you create a stock-up routine that matches their time frame.

Whichever approach you choose, remember that your success rides on your kitchen setup. Organizing your space helps you eliminate unnecessary purchases and avoid food waste (which is a huge money waster). When your food is not sorted and separated properly, it can be difficult to know what you have and what you need, so you can inadvertently purchase unnecessary items. Sales cannot help you save money if your space is unorganized. Be sure to set up your kitchen in a way that enables you to see everything you have on hand easily and quickly, so you can take advantage of sales and save the most money every week.

Organizing the Pantry

When I first created a system for my groceries, I needed it to serve me well. As someone who is always busy and often forgetful, my system had to make it easy for me to see everything at a glance. That meant that I needed to stack like items together, label everything that I took out of their original packaging, and be able to quickly gather items for cooking. This was the only way that my system would be sustainable.

To avoid getting overwhelmed, I started small, organizing one space at a time. I started with my pantry, which, at the time, was one cupboard that had four shelves that were deep and narrow. It was not a lot of space, but I made the most out of it, organizing it to hold my most used items, such as rice, flour, cooking oils, canned food, and snacks.

After organizing the space, I realized that it was not enough for all of my items, so I brainstormed and decided to make over a coat closet that was in the hall just off the kitchen. I went to a home-improvement store, picked up some shelving and supplies, and my husband screwed the shelves in place in just under an hour. Now, I had enough space to organize everything else that my pantry needed to hold.

However you set up your pantry, it needs to serve your needs and make sense to you. If you find that something doesn't work for you, you can always change it.

Using Your Freezer for Bulk Storage

Once I finished organizing my pantries, I went on to my fridge essentials, and eventually focused on my freezer, which revealed a huge potential that I had never noticed before. Freezers are the most underutilized storage spaces in your kitchen, and they are a game changer for organizing food. Moreover, your freezer is incredibly efficient and effective in preserving your stock. Most of us tend to focus on using our pantry to hold much of our stockpile, but I'm telling you, your freezer can do substantially more for you.

Some of my favorite foods to freeze are bread, cheese, hummus, guacamole, meat, broth, seafood (shrimp, crab, fish, and so on), chicken, precooked meat (such as shredded chicken or ground beef), soups (without rice, potato, pasta), nuts, milk, yogurt, banana, grapes, berries, onion, garlic, herbs (I dry them out first to remove the moisture), butter, bacon, sausage, hot dogs, homemade dough (pizza, bread, and so on), nacho cheese, pastries, cookies, cake, pasta sauce, and seeds (pumpkin, sunflower, and so on).

There are plenty of other items you can freeze as well. If you ever wonder what you can freeze, go to the freezer section of your grocery store for more ideas. Anything that is there can be frozen at home.

Just make sure you don't block your freezer's fan and thermostat, and leave a little room for the cold air to flow. That way, you can make the most of your freezer space without blocking the necessary vents from functioning properly.

Creating a Routine That Serves Your System

Once you're done organizing your kitchen space and you have a clear picture of the items that you use most often, it's time to create a solid shopping routine.

Creating a Menu the Right Way

As I mentioned earlier, we shop based on sales, and we stock up on items when they are priced at their lowest. This directly reflects how we create our menu plan for the week. Instead of the typical way most people create a menu plan—which is to add recipes first and then shop for ingredients—you will list out recipes that you can make with food you currently have and food you're going to buy this week on sale. With this method, you'll create budget-friendly meals that were based on items that were purchased at their lowest price, bringing down the per person meal cost and saving you money easily.

Creating Simple Meals

Along the lines of creating meals based on items you have on hand as well as current sales, creating simple meals is a great way to spend less at the grocery store. Having a repertoire of five-ingredient-or-less recipes will not only make it easier for you to pull together a dinner in a matter of minutes, even on a busy weeknight, but it also means that it requires less items to be picked up from the store. When your recipe has minimal ingredients, it's easier to prepare meals and faster to clean up the kitchen later. A good recipe guide that works well is choosing one protein (beef, chicken, beans), two vegetables (broccoli, carrots, zucchini), a starch or carb (rice or pasta), and a cooking fat. It's a great template that you can mix and match based on the items you have on hand. It reminds me of a capsule wardrobe, which is a minimal wardrobe that includes basics that you can mix and match to create numerous outfits quickly and easily. This is the same concept, and it not only saves you time, but money as well. It also makes cooking dinner so much easier, even when you're tired, so you minimize drive-through visits, another win-win.

Setting Aside a Small Stock Budget

If your grocery budget is already limited, you might wonder how you are supposed to afford stocking up when you can barely afford buying the things you need every week. It's a valid point, and I want to address it and give you a strategy that will help. Set aside about twenty dollars from your grocery budget every week or every other week if you are severely limited in funds. As items go on sale and you're ready to stock up, use the money you set aside to buy the extra items. As you get into the habit of stocking up on items when they are at their lowest price, you'll start to save more and more, which frees up more money you can use to stock up. It becomes a snowball effect: The more you save, the more you stock up, which helps you save more. Also, remember to start small with your stockpiling. Maybe you don't stockpile for six to eight weeks the very first time. Instead, you buy one or two extra of the item and slowly build your stockpile until you are able to get enough to hold you through to the next sale. Stockpiling is meant to help you save money, so it's okay to save slowly and gradually.

Labeling Your Ingredients

When I first started buying meat in bulk and separating it into meal-sized portions to freeze, I thought I could recognize what everything would be once it was frozen. Trust me, friend, stew meat and thin steak look the same when they're frozen. I know because I learned that the hard way. I planned for a slow cooker meal, pulled out what I thought was stew meat, and the next morning when it was thawed out, I realized it was steak. I had to create a last-minute recipe switch before heading to work, and it was not fun.

So take it from me and label everything, especially the items you plan to freeze. This way, you know exactly what you are pulling out without having to guess when it's frozen.

Rotating Your Snacks

I like to call this method "snack stack" because you stack your bulk snacks one week at a time. That means that you can still buy your snacks in bulk to save money without having so much of it that your family gets tired of eating the same thing for so long. It's a tactic I use a lot, and it works well. Each week, you will rotate your bulk snacks and only put out enough for a week's worth; once that snack is done, rotate a new snack the following week. It's a great way to keep snack options interesting, especially for kids. This method is very similar to rotating your kids' toys so that they play with them without getting tired of playing with the same toys repeatedly.

Batch-Cooking

Arguably, I've saved the best for last. Batch-cooking is one of my favorite ways to use up what I have, spend less time in the kitchen, and have less cleanup throughout the week. Batch-cooking is different than meal prepping in that you are preparing several different meals for the week, where meal prepping has you eating the same meal every day for a week.

It's a highly productive system of cooking where you cook all your meals for the week in just a couple of hours. It's such a time saver because you essentially use your kitchen tools just once for a few hours on cooking day. Your knife and small appliances, such as your food processor or blender, will only need to be cleaned once at the end of your cooking session, which means less cleanup time on busy weeknights. It's a game changer for getting dinner on the table in less than 20 minutes, from start to finish. Each night, you heat up the meal, make a side dish, and dinner is ready to go. You don't have to stand and actively cook every night of the week anymore, since you did all the heavy lifting on a day that you had more time to spend in the kitchen.

Batch-cooking is also a great way to minimize food waste, since you can use up all the fresh vegetables you bought for the week before they spoil. And once the meals have cooled after cooking, they are stored in your fridge and are ready when you are. This helps you avoid takeout, since usually the thing that makes us visit the drive-through is the lack of motivation to cook after a long day. Now, you don't have to cook an entire meal, but you and your family can still eat a well-balanced dinner you made with ingredients you know. This one method helped me save hundreds of dollars every month, and it's something I do often. On weeks when I don't batch-cook, I feel such a difference in how much effort I have to put into making dinner and how much more work I have to do when I'm tired. It's one of my favorite methods for saving time and money, and it's one I see myself using for decades to come because it works so well!

Here's a quick checklist to help you get started if you want to try batch-cooking yourself.

1. Plan your menu based on what you have on hand.
2. Check your pantry first, and then create your shopping list.
3. Thaw all meat (if any) the night before.
4. Prep your ingredients all at once (chop, slice, shred).
5. Use your burners, oven, and crockpot at the same time.
6. Use a timer so nothing gets burned.
7. Let meals cool completely.
8. Cover well and store in fridge.

To recap, taking small steps to save money on your groceries is key to long-term savings. But to truly amplify your savings and create a routine that works well, you need to create a savings ecosystem that works within your kitchen space. That ecosystem will enable you to strategically stock up on items you need, save money on everything you use, and eliminate food waste by efficiently using up what you have on hand. That, my friend, is a savings ecosystem that helps you thrive.

Part IV

Bill Savings

Chapter 11

Bill Breakdown: Getting to Know Your Bills

When you think of saving money, what is the first expense you decide to cut back on? Most of us tend to start reducing our lifestyle expenses, such as takeout, salon visits, shopping, or brunch with friends. To many, taking control of your finances can sometimes look like getting rid of most of the fun from your budget and just keeping the necessary expenses. What if I told you that you can cut back on your necessary expenses without sacrificing your quality of life?

Your monthly bills, those fixed bills that you pay every single month, while necessary, are a huge part of your overall budget. Typically, these expenses can take up more than 50 percent of your income. And while they are classified as "fixed" in your budget, don't let that label mislead you. There are still several ways you can reduce their effect on your budget without sacrificing their benefits so you can enjoy more financial freedom for you to afford the things you love the most.

Understand the Three Types of Bills

Before we discuss strategies to reduce your bills, we need to first break down the types of bills you have in your budget and what each one provides to the quality of your life. Bills can be separated into three distinct categories. There are essential bills, functional bills, and lifestyle bills:

- Essentials are necessary for your survival, meaning they are vital to your life. These expenses include housing, utilities, phone, groceries, and so on. Whenever you face circumstances where you need to create a bare-bones budget or scale back your budget to only the necessities, these are the expenses that take priority over everything else.

- Functionals are services or products that help you better function in your day-to-day life. Some of those expenses are car insurance, home alarm service, day care, parking permits, Internet (although this can also be classified as essential), and so on.
- Lifestyle expenses are the services that enhance your life by providing comfort, entertainment, and more time. Cable, streaming services, landscaping, cleaning services, meal delivery, grocery pickup, memberships, shopping, entertainment, and subscriptions tend to fall in this category.

Now that you know the types of expenses you are working with, it will be easier for you to determine how to reduce them. For example, with essential and functional expenses, your primary focus would be on making small behavioral changes that can help reduce their cost or switching providers if you have the option. With lifestyle expenses, you have more freedom to pause or cancel services you aren't using or test out more affordable options.

It's important to note that while groceries fall under essential expenses because they're needed for survival, they are managed more similarly to lifestyle expenses, since you typically have much more freedom in choosing which stores you shop, the type of food you buy, and the systems you implement. How much you save on groceries is directly influenced by your lifestyle and routines.

Now that you have a better understanding of the types of expenses you have, let's explore some strategies to help you reduce their cost.

Create Competition for Your Business

As a paying customer, you are incredibly valuable. Although it may sometimes feel like you are just another number in a business's database, companies strive for high customer retention. They want to keep you as a paying customer. So use this knowledge to your advantage. Let companies compete for your business by renegotiating your rates regularly. A good rule of thumb is to negotiate your rates, interest, premiums, and fees every three to six months or when the next rate increase happens, which can be up to 12 months.

And to properly negotiate, you need to first do your research.

1. Know your credit score.
2. Call the competitors, check their websites for promotional offers, and find out what the current rates are in comparison to your provider's rates.
3. Check what your current provider is offering to new customers as well.
4. Check out the promotional offers you're receiving online and by mail.

This information is important information you will use as leverage to help you negotiate a better rate. The more prepared you are, the more confident you are, and the more successful your negotiation efforts will be. You can try this approach when it comes to your telephone, Internet, streaming services, cable TV, credit cards, and other services.

Avoid Payment Autopilot

Listen, automation is a great thing—when used in certain instances, such as automatically contributing to your investments every month. But automating your bill payments is not a good idea in most cases. The reason being that when you automate your payment, you stop looking at your statements and assume that it's all correct. When you don't monitor your statements, you don't notice gradual small upticks that periodically increase your payment amount. In the long run, this can cost you hundreds of dollars more per year. Instead, manage your bills like a company would. A company hires and pays accountants to monitor every bill and manually make the payments because they understand that small spending leaks can lead to financial disaster in the long run.

Similarly, you need to approach your bills with the same care. Take just five minutes to review your statement and understand what you are paying for before making a payment. Check these things:

- Was there in increase in usage on your part?
- Was there a mistake on the bill?
- Did they recently increase their rates?

What's more, don't give any company direct access to your bank account for automatic deductions. No entity should have that much access to your financial accounts. Instead, use your bank's bill pay function to make your payment when you're ready.

Bundle Your Services

A great way to organize your bills is to combine services into one bundle whenever possible. It enables you to pay less per service in exchange for allowing one company to have more of your business. It's a win-win.

But there's a caveat; don't bundle services you don't use for the sake of getting what seems to be a deal that costs just a few dollars more. If it's not a service you use anyway, then this is an upsell from the company and doesn't save you money. It's like buying an item just because it's on sale and not because you truly need it. As long as you avoid extras, bundling your services is an easy way to reduce your monthly bill.

What Deserves Your Money?

Think about the services you currently have and how often you use them. Better yet, think about how their functionality benefits you. For example, do you really need a landline? Probably not. Many people make monthly payments for services that they probably don't use as often as they intended to.

This was something that took a bit of finessing for me and my husband when we were paying off debt and trying to reduce our expenses. We had to take a hard look at some of our bills and decide if those services were really worth their cost in serving us. We started with our cable bill. Friend, I did not want to cut the cable because I was afraid that I would have nothing good to watch on TV. But we decided to cancel cable for a couple of months to test it out and see if it would make a difference in our day-to-day life. Knowing that we were doing a trial run without cable brought my anxiety level way down because I thought, "It's only temporary; if I absolutely hate not having cable, I can always pay to turn it back on."

But something magical happened. The shows I loved watching on HGTV and Food Network were quickly replaced with a network station called Create by PBS. They had cooking shows, travel shows, and even HGTV-style shows. And I found myself really enjoying those just as much as I did with Food Network and HGTV. As for the kiddos, they loved watching Netflix shows on demand, and PBS also filled the gap. I also realized that we only watched TV for about an hour a day because we were so busy.

So after a couple of months, I couldn't imagine paying $110 per month again for cable. And it's been more than 12 years since! That's $15,840 we've saved just by challenging our monthly bills and trying something new.

The truth is we all get used to paying for things we don't even use, but we don't take the time to assess their value in our life. Take a moment and try this:

1. Jot down some of your monthly lifestyle expenses. For example, two adults have gym memberships for $50 per month for a combined total of $100.
2. Write down how many times you typically use them in a month. Due to busy schedules, one person goes to the gym twice a month, and the other person doesn't go at all.
3. Then, take the total monthly bill and divide it by the number of times you use it for the month. $100 divided by 2 visits = $50 per gym visit.

Is the amount you're paying per usage worth it?

This will help you figure out what expenses aren't really serving you right now, and you can choose to pause them, reduce the membership level, or cut them out altogether. Now, remember, just because you cut something out doesn't mean that you can't get it back if you change your mind. But you may surprise yourself when you find out that some of those "needs" weren't really enhancing your life that much. Not enough for it to be worth your money anyway. By doing this, you can free up money for the things you enjoy using.

So start assessing your usage. Keep what serves you and get rid of anything that doesn't. You'll free up more money, and you'll have more gratitude for the things you've kept on your list.

You Can Even Reduce Your Utilities Payment

Reducing your energy costs can save you a lot of money each month. But not at the expense of creating discomfort. So here are some things you can consider if you want to reduce your monthly energy expenses. One simple step is to research what the optimal temperature settings are for your region. A good balance is adjusting your temperature even just one or two degrees slightly closer to the range that your utility company suggests as optimal. I live in California and personally get cold easily, so I'm generally comfortable with my thermostat set at 76–78 degrees in the summer and 70 degrees in the winter. I prefer it to be a little warmer. Suggested settings in my area are 78 degrees in the summer and 68 degrees in the winter.

You can also cut your water bill by watching your usage. Do you let the water run for a long time when you're brushing your teeth? Are your showers longer than they need to be? Do you run the faucet nonstop when you're doing dishes? Do you have a timer on your gardening hose, and is it wasting more water than necessary? You'd be surprised how quickly unnecessary water usage adds up in dollars.

A great resource is your energy provider's website. There are usually helpful articles and suggestions to help you cut costs while staying comfortable by doing things such as making sure you don't leave lights and TVs turned on in rooms when no one is there. You may also find some incentive and rebate programs that reward you when you use your appliances at non-peak usage times, reduce thermostat settings, and so on.

Reducing Your Debt

In most cases, credit cards fall under lifestyle bills because they're typically the result of impulse purchases and lifestyle enhancements or luxuries. And if you're in the process of paying off your credit cards right now, these next few tips will help you reduce some of those costs so you can pay off those cards easier and quicker. You might think that your credit card terms can't be negotiated, but let me tell you, friend, there is a lot you can do to give you some breathing room with your credit cards. Numbers such as your interest rate, annual fee, and even your monthly payment amount can be negotiated. And let me quickly explain what those numbers look like so we're on the same page.

Your interest rate is the percentage that the bank charges you based on your total balance, when you don't pay your balance in full each month. So let's say you have a card with an interest rate of 14% APR, which is the annual percentage rate, and your balance on that card is $1,000 right now. The bank would take your rate and divide that by 365 to get the daily interest charge, which in this case, comes out to 0.00038356. Then, they multiply that crazy-looking number with your current balance of $1,000 to get $0.38356164, which is the daily interest charge. Finally, they multiply that daily interest charge by 30 days to get $11.51, which is the monthly interest charged. You don't have to calculate all that to know that interest charges are hefty and add up quickly. So if you can negotiate a lower interest rate, that saves you money, and those extra savings can pay off your debt even faster!

You can even negotiate to get your credit card annual fees waived. Some credit cards offer special perks in exchange for charging an annual fee. These annual fees can be anywhere between $95 to $695. Many of the airline credit cards are set up with annual fees in order to enjoy the perks of mile bonuses.

A little later, in Chapter 13, we'll explain the reason why credit card companies are willing to negotiate terms with you and what steps to take to increase your chance of success. For now, just know that, in many cases, all these numbers are negotiable.

Utilize Balance Transfer Promotions

Balance transfer offers are another great way to reduce your overall debt payments and accelerate your payoff date. A balance transfer offer is essentially when a creditor will allow you to transfer your debt from another credit card onto their card, and they provide a temporary 0% interest rate for 12–18 months. This is a great way for you to pay off your debt, interest free! This is how my husband and I were able to accelerate our debt payoff, and it saved us literally thousands of dollars overall.

This chapter by no means covers every possible option or strategy to save money on your bills. But these strategies provide a great starting point to get you well on your way to reducing your monthly expenses without sacrificing your lifestyle or the quality of the services you receive. Remember, your goal of saving money is to be able to afford more of the things that matter so you can truly live your best life.

Chapter 12
The Benefits of a Bill Routine

Taking control of your finances is not a one-and-done occurrence. Rather, it is a set of systems and routines that enable you to manage your money on a consistent, ongoing basis. Your bill routine is a necessary player in your financial team. Set up correctly, your routine can create financial peace and stability.

Most of us are creatures of habit: We thrive off familiar schedules and tasks that help give us structure and goals to meet in our day to day. For this reason, creating routines provides a sense of comfort because we know that we can complete each task without much effort, like brushing our teeth or putting on deodorant. It becomes a pattern of behavior that builds muscle memory over time and provides a method we can confidently rely on to be more efficient while staying on track.

Why Is a Routine Important?

A routine is merely a pattern of several behavioral steps that allows us to optimize our life administrative functions. Life administrative tasks are those necessary actions that we take every single month that maintain stability with our health and well-being as well as our finances. For example, buying groceries every week keeps you and your family fed. Washing your clothes and cleaning your home maintains a clean and healthy environment for you (and your body) to reside in. Taking a shower and regular grooming are also necessary to maintain good hygiene and arguably the most basic terms of healthy living. All these tasks are very necessary components of leading a healthy life in the most basic terms.

Similarly, your bill routine is a necessary part of your financial hygiene and helps you maintain basic financial health. And you might not have realized it, but you already have a bill routine in place. I promise you, if you look closely, there is a behavioral pattern that you have when it comes to paying your bills every month.

Whether or not your bill routine was mindfully created, efficient, or helping you streamline your finances is a different story. Some of you might pay your bills as soon as you receive your statement. Some of you might forget to pay until they send you a second notice. And some of you feel like you're in a constant cycle of due date frenzy, always wondering what today's date is and frantically checking if anything was due that you need to quickly pay. It all feels a bit chaotic and out of control. And yet, you continue with this routine, even though it adds unnecessary stress. Regardless of what your current bill routine is, improving it will bring more balance to your finances and your life.

The Benefits of Creating an Intentional Bill Routine

Your bill routine needs to be created with intention. It needs to provide structure that you can rely on to keep track of your bills without additional effort on your part. Once you set up a solid system, it will keep your bills organized so you don't have to think about it. To maintain it and keep it moving, your only job is to set aside five to ten minutes every month or every two weeks and schedule out your bill payments. And you can do this by going to your bank's website and using their bill pay function or going directly to the payee's website and scheduling the payment there. Either way, planning and scheduling your payments ahead of time keeps you in control. You can stop feeling stressed because of looming due dates or late payment fees and you can stop feeling anxious that your service might be interrupted because of a missed payment.

A solid bill routine takes away the anxiety and replaces it with peace of mind. It is there to make it easier for you to take control of your monthly responsibilities without having to keep it all in your head. This kind of routine gives you freedom.

Spotting and Removing Unwanted Charges

Whether you have a system that supports your financial health or creates chaos every month, it's the consistency that drives the impact. With an intentional bill payment routine, you'll have more opportunities to review your charges, fix corrections, and just be aware of what you are paying.

Having that time and space to review your bills helps you avoid paying for charges that were added incorrectly or without your knowledge. Too often, people pay their bills in such a rush that they don't take the time to review what they are paying, and later they discover that they've been overpaying for months and sometimes years. Companies know that many of their customers are so busy that they might not check their statements thoroughly, so they periodically increase their rates or fees knowing that most clients won't notice.

Only those who spot these changes will have the opportunity to call and ask the provider for more information and request for the increases to be reversed or reduced, saving them money and reducing future bills. Generally, companies will not send out notices for minor increases, so it's important to be alert and stay proactive when checking your charges before you make your payment. When you call up your service provider and question your bill charges, you protect your wallet. Taking a few moments to do this can free up more money—to improve your finances and enhance your life.

Assessing Which Services Actually Serve You

Your payment routine also does something amazing for you. Because all your bills are organized, you get a mini snapshot of all your bills each month. That's a natural plus to having a system, but that's not the amazing part. Your routine gives you the chance to periodically assess your payments to see which services actually serve you in your current season of life. As you pay your car wash subscription every month, you'll probably start asking yourself if you use that service enough for it to be worth the monthly payment. If you paid the gym membership for the last three months and have only gone to the gym twice during that period, it will prompt you to decide whether or not you want to cancel your membership. When you can assess your services and cut out things that don't work well for you, you protect your money and become more intentional with how you choose to spend it.

Improving Your Credit Score

Paying your bills on time means you'll improve your credit as well. Your credit card and loan payments are bills too. And when you consistently pay them on time, you avoid late fees, but more importantly, your on-time payments are reported to the credit bureaus, and your credit score improves as a result. Creditors are more likely to give you a better interest rate when they can see a strong track record of timely payments because that means you are a low-risk borrower, one who probably won't default on their payments based on payment history. Improving your credit score is a huge deal in saving money! How? If you have good credit (a high credit score), you qualify for better interest rates on money you borrow, so you pay less interest.

Let me break it down for you.

Rachel has a credit score of 720, and Tammy has a credit score of 620. If each borrower took out a five-year car loan of $20,000 and put $1,000 toward the down payment, how much would each borrower pay back with interest? Let's look at Figure 12.1 to see how it plays out over five years.

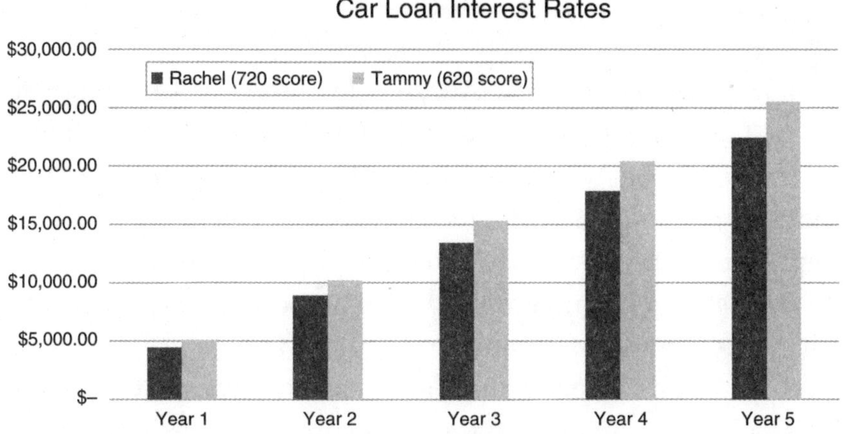

Figure 12.1

Rachel qualified for a 6.85% APR while Tammy qualified for 12.38% APR on the loan. Tammy's rate is nearly double that of Rachel's. Based on the chart, Tammy's payments are visibly greater than Rachel's, and the gap between their payment totals continues to increase with each year.

As we look at Figure 12.2, we can see that over the span of five years, Tammy paid $3,120 more than Rachel for the same exact car. By the time we get to year 4, Tammy has already paid more than her original $20,000 loan. That essentially means that year 5 payments represent the total amount she paid in interest over the life of the loan, which was a whopping $5,560. That's not even considering the initial $1,000 down payment. So Tammy paid a total of $26,560 for her car. Rachel, on the other hand, paid

	Rachel (720 score)	Tammy (620 score)	Variance
Year 1	$ 4,488.00	$ 5,112.00	$ 624.00
Year 2	$ 8,976.00	$ 10,224.00	$ 1,248.00
Year 3	$ 13,464.00	$ 15,336.00	$ 1,872.00
Year 4	$ 17,952.00	$ 20,448.00	$ 2,496.00
Year 5	$ 22,440.00	$ 25,560.00	$ 3,120.00

Figure 12.2

a total of $2,440 in interest over the life of the loan and a total of $23,440 for her car, including the initial $1,000 down payment.

Imagine what you could do with an extra $3,120 in your pocket. I bet you can think of a few areas in your finances that could benefit from an extra three grand and some change. And this is just one example of how much you can save when you organize your bills and improve your credit score.

Keep in mind that in this particular example we were looking at a car loan, which is based on a simple interest rate model, meaning that you pay the exact same interest amount every month for the life of the loan and the interest does not compound from one month to another, as it does with a credit card balance. So if you could save this much money on a simple interest loan, imagine how much you can save on compound interest. This is why it's so vital that you take care of your credit, and a major part of that is maintaining a healthy bill payment system that allows you to keep track of your bills and help you consistently make your payments on time every month.

Each Step Matters

Remember, each part or area of your finances affects the other areas, and each step within a particular area helps create momentum that works like the domino effect, as we mentioned in Chapter 1. When the steps allow one part to work well, all the financial parts stand strong and aligned, but when one is flawed, they can all come tumbling down. This is why creating systems that build a solid structure and foundation for your finances is so important to your overall financial health. These systems keep you organized and in control, which helps you save money without much effort.

Setting up a bill routine saves time, energy, and money. It's one of those tasks that you set up once and it serves you forever, with some minor tweaks and changes along the way, of course. This one small task has the power to substantially impact your finances without disrupting your life. Setting up a routine to pay your monthly bills has a very high ROI (return on investment): You spend minimal effort and get to reap ongoing benefits.

As Easy as 1-2-3

Setting up a bill routine is easy and takes just three steps. The first step is to set up your payment method. My favorite is setting up bill payments through the bank. It's a brain dump of all your bills so that you don't have to try to keep it straight in your head. Instead, your bank will essentially keep it organized for you automatically. Once your payment dates, amounts, and vendor or provider information are added, you're well on your way to saving time and energy every month because your bank is now your new assistant, taking care of everything with your supervision. The process to set up bill payment with your bank takes about thirty minutes to an hour to do the initial set up. A one-time setup, and you're ready to go!

The second step is to create a monthly payment calendar that you can use with your budget so you can stay on track. This takes about five minutes to complete since you are just filling your calendar with your bill payment due dates, which happen to be the same each month.

The third step is to take five to ten minutes each month reviewing your bill charges and scheduling your payments with the bank or directly with the vendor. That's it, friend. That's the entire routine.

Maintaining this system is quite easy as well. As you acquire new services or bills, you simply log in to your bank account and add them to your bill pay or go to the service provider and set up a payment account. Easy-peasy.

It's a system that builds a foundation within your financial structure that you can rely on for literally decades. And it will work like a well-oiled machine so that as you feed it information once a month, it does the work for you. It makes the payment, generates your receipt, keeps track of how much you've paid in total, and provides data and insight to help you make better decisions with how you direct your money. That means you have total control and the power to adjust and change as you need to, and that's the perfect balance you need. Full control without the heavy burden of taking care of everything on your own. Your system does the lifting for you; you just need to do your part and maintain it well.

Simplicity Provides Ease

Setting up a bill routine is so simple yet so impactful. Gone are the days of bills that continue to pile on your kitchen table and cause you stress and anxiety. This simple system helps to declutter your home from unnecessary mail, streamline a part of your finances since you'll schedule everything just once a month, and shorten your to-do list from all the small, distracting tasks that you used to complete several times a month. Your financial system has efficiency built in, and it's a step that crosses off half a dozen steps as a result.

Countless benefits are attached to these very small steps, making this *my* kind of financial planning and management. It's what my husband and I, look for the most. A system that turns down the busy-ness dial just a little and that keeps us organized and on top of our financial responsibilities without disrupting our day-to-day life. A system that helps ease my mind, calm the chaos that often comes with paying bills, and ensures that we pay our bills on time, every month with consistency, and positively impacts my credit and financial standing as a whole? Yes, please!

Chapter 13
Saving Money on Your Debt Payments

It's no surprise that debt, especially consumer debt that is accompanied by compound interest charges, is detrimental to your financial health. What is shocking is how quickly your debt can escalate if you're not careful. When my husband and I accumulated our debt, it happened so subtly that I didn't realize how monumental our debt balance had become until I took time to add up the totals. The number sent my heartbeat into pounding-out-of-my-chest mode.

Debt can feel debilitating when you feel stuck and aren't sure how to take control of it. So it's important to spot the areas of your debt that are still in your control. One area is your debt repayment plan. When my husband and I sat down together to create our plan of action, we focused on methods that could help us save money on interest and accelerate our payoff time frame. Our goal was to pay off our debt as fast as we could so that we could remove the burden and pay as little interest as possible. We indeed found methods that worked to help us achieve our goal. And these methods focused on our "circle of influence."

The Circle of Influence

The "circle of influence" is an idea that Steven Covey crafted in his book *The 7 Habits of Highly Effective People*, published in 1989, which further explored the concept of the "locus of control." The idea of the "locus of control" (which was first introduced in 1954 by American psychologist Julian Rotter) refers to how much control you believe you have over your behavior. The "circle of influence" concept takes that idea one step further, by looking at the degree of how much you believe that *your* actions and decisions impact your outcomes. It further explains that people who focus on their circle of influence before taking action tend to be more proactive because they believe their actions directly reflect how successful they are with achieving their goals.

The strategies my husband and I chose helped us focus on our circle of influence, which, in the case of our debt, were the changes *we* could make to take better control of our spending, creating a game plan to pay more toward our debt to save time and money in the process.

Improve Your Credit

In Chapter 12, "The Benefits of a Bill Routine," we talked about how beneficial it is to improve your credit for future purchases and lower interest rates. But improving your credit will also help you save money while you are paying off your debt now.

One quick and easy way to improve your credit standing is by reviewing your credit report and fixing any errors you find. It's important that you obtain your credit report from the official reporting agencies (at the time of this writing, the bureaus are Experian, Equifax, and TransUnion). Once you receive your report, search for common, overlooked errors such as incorrect credit limit, incorrect spellings of your name, lines of credit that aren't yours, and so on. Then, write an email to the credit bureaus explaining in detail what errors need to be fixed and provide proper documentation to prove that the information you are providing is correct. They are required to respond to your email in 30 days, so be sure to follow up every 30 days until your issue is resolved.

Negotiate Your Interest Rates

As we discussed in Chapter 11, some of your credit card terms are negotiable, even when you are in debt. You can request to reduce your current interest rates, especially if you have a track record of making your payments on time. Let's look at the bigger picture to see why this is possible. You *are* a valued, paying customer to the bank. You make your payments on time, and you are loyal and have been with this bank for years and are likely to do business with them in the future by way of new accounts, credit cards, loans, and so on. From the bank's standpoint, you are a customer they want to keep for the long term. Banks take customer satisfaction so seriously that many of them have a specialized customer retention department dedicated to keeping their customers happy, which can sometimes mean reducing your interest rate to keep you around longer.

But before you rush to ask for a reduced rate, you need to do your research so you can create a good case that gets approved. Here are some steps that my husband and I took that made it easier for us to negotiate our rates:

- **Know your credit score:** Your credit score is a good indicator to lenders (i.e., your bank) whether you are a high-risk or low-risk borrower. And this directly impacts your chances of reducing your interest rate. Lenders generally do not want to reduce interest charges for a borrower they deem to be higher risk. And as we discussed in Chapter 12, lower credit scores typically mean higher risk, which translates to higher interest charges to help offset some of that risk.
- **Know your offers:** Check current offers, preapprovals that were emailed or mailed to you, and any competitor sign up

bonuses as well. This does a couple of things. First, it shows that you are a valued and sought-after borrower, which encourages your current lender to retain you as a customer. And second, it shows your lender that you have other options but are choosing loyalty to them first, which gives you a much better chance to have your request granted.

- **Know your bank's offers to new customers:** Understanding what current offers your bank is providing to their new customers is intel you can use for your benefit. Since it's a current offer, it's likely easier to use for customer retention efforts as well.

While your request is not guaranteed to be granted, these steps do help make it easier for your lender to consider granting your request. The reason being that you provided data that helps make their decision-making process easier.

Hardship Relief Programs

While a hardship relief program is not generally the most common route taken to save money, it is one that is available to you in times of struggle. And it's one that I've personally used and am incredibly grateful for because in my early 20s, I found myself needing to take this route. At the time, my life was flipped upside down, and this took a toll on my finances. In a matter of one month, I filed for a restraining order and divorce after surviving domestic violence, quickly relocated myself and my infant daughter to live with my brother and be close to family, and quit my job for safety reasons. In the midst of all this, I justifiably was not focused on my credit card payments, and as a result, I fell behind. After receiving a phone call from the bank's collections department, I shared my circumstances, and the representative not only consoled me but let me know about its hardship program. I eagerly requested to be enrolled, and my bank happily worked with me to create a payment plan that I could handle. It was just what I needed to catch my breath and get back on track.

Most banks generally offer a hardship relief program to help you pay down your balance when you start to fall behind or become delinquent in your payments. Their incentive is to recoup as much of their money as possible, so they are willing to work with you if you provide documentation that can prove your current hardship.

These programs can help reduce your minimum payment, reduce your interest rate, create a customized payment plan, or pause your interest temporarily. Each program has a different set of criteria and is structured differently, so it's best to contact your bank or lender directly to know your options.

The steps we've discussed so far in this chapter help you take better control of your credit and debt health. These initial steps are small but have a big impact on the goal of becoming debt free. They help build the necessary foundation to create a debt payment game plan that works with your situation, yielding more progress than implementing a cookie-cutter framework. With the first steps taken, you can create a tailored plan that empowers you to make more progress toward debt freedom with more ease.

Creating a Debt Payoff Game Plan

There is an art to paying off debt efficiently and cost-effectively, and that art lies in your game plan. For your game plan to work well and help you reach success, it must be realistic. And that means you need to know some important numbers.

Know Your Numbers

The first step in taking action with your debt payoff game plan is to know your numbers:

- **Your debt total:** Your plan needs to reflect your total debt as of today, not an estimation. Creating a plan based on estimated numbers can create uncertainty, confusion, and lack of confidence. When you know what your exact debt total is, it enables you to take the right steps the first time, without hesitation.
- **Your net income:** As you create your budget and learn your spending patterns, you'll also learn how much money you can set aside each month to be used to pay your debt. How much you spend each month and how much debt you pay off are directly linked. Your budget is a key factor in helping you pay off your debt because it's the tool that keeps you in control of your spending. And when you can control your spending, you ultimately free up money in your budget so that you can then pay off more debt.
- **Your interest rates:** Each piece of debt you owe is tied to an interest rate. So make a simple list with the name of each debt, the total balance, and its interest rate.

Pick Your Payment Method

There are two popular methods to pay off your debt. Regardless of the method you choose, you will essentially focus on paying off one piece of debt at a time while making minimum payments on all your other debt. Let's talk about both methods and weigh out the pros and cons.

- **Avalanche method:** Pay your debt down based on the highest interest rate first. With this method, you save a lot of money in interest, and you accelerate your debt payoff in the long run. The con is that it requires a little more discipline because you don't get as many dopamine hits with quick wins.

- **Snowball method:** Pay the smallest balance first and ignore the interest rate. This method offers quick wins along the way, which helps with motivation. But you're paying more interest than is necessary.

The best method for you depends on your personality and what gets you more excited: quick wins or saving time and money.

My husband and I personally used the debt avalanche method to pay off our debt because saving money was more important to us than quick wins, and it helped us pay off our debt much faster. This is the method I suggest to anyone who asks for my opinion on the matter because ultimately, I want you to pay off your debt with less money, and the avalanche method achieves that. That said, one more approach if you have a lot of different debts would be to start with the snowball method to knock out a couple of quick easy debts so you have an early taste of success and then switch to the avalanche method for everything else to really get more material results.

Track Your Debt Payments

Creating a plan is the easy part; the hard part is the follow-through. Tracking your payments keeps you focused and accountable for the plan you created. When you regularly check in, it allows you to see your progress and gives you motivation to continue moving forward.

Tracking creates a habit that helps you stay on a plan, even when life gets busy. An easy way to track is using a debt tracker. This can be a sheet of paper, an Excel spreadsheet, or a sheet that you can make part of your budget planner (I used the latter). This helps you stay organized and enables you to visually see your progress every month.

Be Consistent

Remember what we talked about in the earlier chapters: Whatever you do consistently will create momentum. So use consistency to help you build a solid habit and routine that pushes you forward, even when you are feeling tired and discouraged.

Adjust as Necessary

I'm a huge proponent that with every plan, there must be a margin of space where you can allow for adjustments. This flexibility helps you recognize what works and what needs to be edited from the plan, and in the long run, this is what ultimately helps you reach your goals. There is no sense in being rigid.

I say that now, but when I first started on my financial journey, I had a standard of perfectionism that choked my progress. I would get frustrated if I made a mistake, if I overspent slightly, or if I wasn't seeing what I viewed as impressive results. This strictness is what I view now as narrow-mindedness; I was simply not open to the possibility that I could try other ways to see if something worked better for me or that perhaps some of the failures I faced were from the method and not my lack of discipline. The bottom line is that rigidity does not help anyone. It only makes it harder for you to experiment and discover your optimal plan.

There will be many times during your plan where you might find your seasons of life change, and that is the exact moment when your plan must follow suit and change as well. Otherwise, you will be attempting to squeeze a square peg into a round hole.

It simply will not work. So instead of wasting time trying to make it fit, spend time thinking of how to change the shape of your plan so it easily glides into place and supports your goals while working with your lifestyle, not against it.

Recap of the Game Plan

With debt being such a major pain point for so many people, I think it is necessary to recap our game plan so you can get started easily. Here's a quick checklist of what a successful debt payoff game plan looks like:

- Know your numbers;
- Pick your payment method;
- Track your debt payments;
- Be consistent;
- Adjust as necessary.

As you can see from the checklist, every step relies on your situation, your preferences, and your capabilities. It is not a cookie-cutter approach that you are forced to fit into your life; rather, it provides the principles that help you assess where you are, address how to move forward, and amplify your effort so you can pay off your debt while saving time and money along the way.

This system works because it's based on small steps and doesn't require drastic disruption of your life. And that's the beauty of small steps: They create massive impact without severe lifestyle changes. They take you from point A to point B gradually, so you don't feel overwhelmed in the process. Feeling overwhelmed creates mental obstacles, but small steps create confidence because of their simplicity.

Your debt payoff plan works best with small action steps that you take daily, not big leaps that feel hard and intimidating. Debt is already stressful—no need to have a plan that unnecessarily adds to the stress. Instead, your plan should provide peace of mind, structure to help you make progress, and empowerment, enabling you to move along your path with better control.

Part V

Budget Better

Chapter 14
Where to Aim Your Focus

If you're just starting to think about your financial health, you might feel flustered in trying to figure out where to focus first. Do you cut your spending, pay off all your debt, or save for an emergency fund? It all seems critically important, and you may not be sure which one to start with or which will make the biggest impact right now. It also might feel uncertain if choosing one area over the other would hinder your efforts altogether.

So how do you choose?

The first thing to remember is that small steps are what make the biggest impact. This means that if you are moving forward, even slowly, you are making progress with your financial goals. To determine which goals to work on first, let's think about our options:

- Creating a budget helps you get organized with your spending and makes you aware of spending leaks and how far your income stretches. It also helps you plan how much to spend and how much to save every month.
- Paying off debt frees up money that you can use in other areas of your life. It also alleviates one of the biggest areas of stress and minimizes the amount of bills you pay each month.
- Saving for an emergency fund gives you peace of mind knowing you are covered in a worst-case scenario that pops up out of the blue. It also helps you eliminate the need to use debt to cover those costs.

It is clear that focusing on any of these options would help you move forward with your money goals. With this micro-level planning, you can achieve your goals, but what if you took it a step further and planned on the macro level? Sure, looking at your current situation and creating a plan of action to move one step forward is a great option. But what if you took a step back and looked at the whole picture, from where you are now to where you want to be? How much more impactful would your steps be if you could create a plan that gives you clarity for each step so you know the purpose of the action that you're taking?

Macro can be defined as a single plan that expands into a set of smaller plans to get to a particular goal. By popular definition, macro focuses on large scale. This may sound counterintuitive to include in a book where we've been working to prove that small scale is better and more impactful. But the beauty is that macro, while it focuses on the big, employs a series of smaller steps to form the big-picture goal. And small steps work best when they are backed by the bigger picture, which provides the road map to make the small steps go in the right direction.

In Chapter 1, "Big Goals Don't Budge," we talked in detail about how it is incredibly difficult to achieve your goals when they are too big. That still holds true here: When the goals are too big, you are encouraged to take big leaps to achieve those goals. When you implement big ideas with big steps, the tasks can become intimidating and overwhelming, eventually stopping you from making progress. What we're proposing here is having big goals work with small steps. That's how macro planning works its magic.

Thus, you will aim your focus on the big goals rather than singular areas of your finances. Instead of focusing on just your emergency fund or paying off debt, focus on the areas that cover a lot of ground with one plan of action. The step will still be small in terms of ease, but it will help you make a big stride forward because it sets the system that will put the singular areas in place so that all is working together like a well-oiled machine.

I have found the following areas highly impactful:

- Creating a budget that prioritizes what you want to include rather than what you need to remove (add versus delete);
- Focusing on your income-producing assets;
- Deciding how and when to automate to your advantage.

Each area tackles several smaller areas that will be addressed as we dive deeper into each macro area.

Create Your Budget That Prioritizes *You*

Most personal finance experts recommend starting here. And while it feels like a small step, its impact is quite the contrary. Creating a budget affects a great number of areas of your finances all at once. But it's important to remember to create flexible budget, one that prioritizes you, the things you want, and the goals you want to achieve, so that it can begin filtering out the areas that need to be eliminated from your spending. Let's take a closer look.

- **It organizes your money:** You have better vision of what is coming in and what is going out.
- **It puts a spotlight on the spending leaks:** It shows you exactly where most of your money is going so you can make the necessary changes to correct it. When you can fix your spending leaks, you can free up more money to direct toward your goals and wants.
- **It helps you take control:** You get a say where your money is directed every time you are paid.
- **It helps you plan ahead:** You can save for emergencies and set-and-get funds for major purchases or expenses, as well as build wealth through long-term investing. It gives you the

space to determine how much of your money you can allocate for these purposes.

- **It eliminates money wasters:** This is different than your spending leaks. These are the monthly expenses that you pay almost on autopilot without much thought. Those payments have been a regular part of your month, and up until this point, you never had a chance to review their value in your life. With a budget, you'll be able to easily recognize when certain services are no longer serving you well; because you will include them in your budget every month, eventually you will be prompted to consider their value. And you may find that some are no longer worth your money, which means you can cancel them and put that money into more important areas of your finances.
- **It accelerates your debt payoff:** With proper budgeting, you will free up money that you can use to pay off more debt in less time.
- **It helps you save more money:** When you can see all your expenses in one place, you'll notice the areas, such as groceries or shopping, where you can begin making small changes to help you save money.

As you can see, focusing your aim on one main area, such as budgeting, greatly impacts so many areas of your finances without overwhelming you in the process. It is a macro move, one that takes some planning but is still structured in small steps that make it easy to take action and make progress consistently.

Focus on Increasing Your Income-producing Assets

Listen, friend, there's only so much you could reasonably cut out of your spending. And while reducing your expenses is a necessary place to begin gaining control over your finances, it's imperative that you also address the other side of the coin, increasing your income. Your income massively impacts your lifestyle choices. And now that you've mastered how to manage your money, it's time to generate more. With that, we need to aim our focus on our income-producing assets, which is a fancy way of saying, any skills, talents, or investment opportunities that can provide additional income for us. That can be our skill set for our career, investing in real estate that generates rental income, and skills we can learn easily to help us generate more money.

In the financial space, there is often talk about diversification. Diversification basically means to differentiate or, to put it more loosely, to have different buckets for the same overall purpose. For example, when you diversify your groceries, you put eggs on one shelf, vegetables in the right drawer, fruit in the left drawer, and milk in the door or on the bottom shelf toward the back. Your groceries are all in the fridge, but they are divided into different areas of your fridge. We can also diversify our groceries by putting some items in the fridge, others in the freezer, and others in the pantry. They are all still groceries, but diversifying where we place them enables us to prolong their shelf life so we have more time to consume them. Diversifying gives us the edge to enjoy our groceries while we strategically avoid food waste.

Diversifying is often mentioned in discussions about investing, for example, diversifying your stocks or your investment portfolio. It is a solid strategy that allows you to reduce your risk of loss because you are not putting all your eggs into one basket. So if one stock plunges, you don't lose all your money because you have other stocks that might go up, essentially balancing out your losses.

This same theory of diversification can and should be applied to your income streams. Most people have a nine-to-five job as their sole source of income. That could be dangerous to your financial health. With just one income stream, you are at a very high risk of financial hardship if you lose your job, which can happen in many different scenarios, such as if the company goes bankrupt, your department restructures the positions, or the economy goes into a recession. With your job being the only reliable income source, you are vulnerable, and you will always be at the mercy of your employer's decisions.

In order to help safeguard your financial health and give you more freedom of choice, you must diversify your income. You can do this by increasing the number of income-producing assets that you have and making them work for you to provide additional sources of monthly income.

Let's look at some ideas to help you get started.

Master Your Current Skills

While you shouldn't solely rely on your job, you should still do what you can to get paid well while you're there. Ask your employer for more training and certification opportunities if that is an option. If it is not an option, then seek training on your own to refine and master your current skill set so you can be the best at what you do. With greater skills, you can apply for higher-paying jobs in your field and earn more money.

Learn New Skills

On your time off, take time to learn one new skill that can help amplify your resume and give you more opportunities for growth. That can be reading books in the field, attending a free class, watching YouTube videos that go in depth on the topic, or finding free online courses that provide certificates of completion.

These are just a few ideas, but there are countless ways to learn new things in today's technologically advanced world; you have a plethora of options to choose from.

Along the same lines of learning new skills for career growth is learning new skills to start a side hustle that can eventually turn into a small business. Even one talent or skill can translate into a service you can offer to others in exchange for a price, which increases your overall monthly income.

Start a Small Business

You might already have a talent or skill that you enjoy doing as a hobby. Is there something you do better than others, something that you get complimented on from friends and family, or something that you do that can help someone else who doesn't have the time to do it themselves?

- If you are a great cook and are great at making big batches of delicious food, you can turn that into a local meal plan service for people who don't have time or talent to cook but don't want to resort to takeout.
- If you love dogs and you have an hour every afternoon that you can dedicate to walking dogs, then you can start a dog-walking service for your neighborhood to help owners who don't have the time to walk their dog. Or you can start a dog-sitting service for people who don't want to leave their pups alone all day while they are at work or on vacation or on a business trip.

Arguably, the hardest part is recognizing the talent or skill you have. Oftentimes, we don't think that what we do is that special, so we discount it in our minds. But you may be able to do something easily that others find difficult. You would be doing a disservice to yourself and those you would help if you discounted all that you could offer.

Investing in an Income-producing Property

Purchasing a property that you can rent out is a great way to increase your long-term wealth and increase your monthly income. Sure, there are risks associated with investing in real estate, as there are with the stock market. But if you buy a property you can afford and hold it for the long term, you can generate what is known as a cash cow over time. A "cash cow" is a term that refers to an asset of any kind (like those we mentioned in this chapter) that provides a steady income or profit for you. You can use the property to produce income for you in several ways:

- Renting it out monthly for residential purposes.
- Renting it out for content creators or companies to use for photoshoots, filming, and so on.
- If the property is near places such as stadiums, beaches, tourist areas, or major work areas such as hospitals or downtown, you can rent it out per day. At the time of this book writing, some of the popular platforms to post your short-term rentals are Airbnb, Vrbo, Booking.com, HomeAway, and so on.

Investing in Funds That Pay Dividends

This is another generally riskier option but one that can potentially provide a solid monthly income. While this book is not financial advice, especially for investing, I wanted to include this option because it is one that has proven to be fruitful in my own personal finance journey. My husband and I have index funds that have dividends, and while at this moment, we are choosing to have those dividends reinvested, we can choose to have those dividends be paid out to us instead.

Do your research and determine what fund would be best for you based on your risk aversion, investment timeline, and your research findings.

How and When to Automate

Previously, we discussed that automation can sometimes be a harmful habit. Automating our bills, for example, can lead to us not paying attention to rate increases, incorrect charges, fraudulent activity, and so on.

However, automation can still be an integral part of your finances when used properly. Automation can help you save money, grow your long-term wealth, and take one task off your to-do list. Let's take a closer look at each of these three strategies.

Saving money is a task that often gets left behind as we tackle our finances. To be clear, the "money saving" I'm referring to here is the literal act of putting money into our savings account, not saving money on expenses such as groceries or our Internet bill. This task is often the least of our priorities. We usually start with reducing expenses, paying off debt, and maybe adding in some money for our coffee run or shopping trip. But savings seems to always come after everything else, and when there isn't any money left, we push the task to the next month.

For this reason, setting up a savings automation will be a game changer for your savings goals. It will be taken out automatically as soon as your salary posts to your bank account. That way, it's out of sight and out of mind, so you can't "accidentally" spend it on something else. This eliminates the barrier of wrestling with monthly decision-making about saving, because the decision has already been made, the amount is predetermined, and the date is set. Everything is in place, and there is nothing additional that needs to be done on our end. We can set this task once and forget about it with no extra effort on our part.

This same approach can be used for our emergency savings and/or miscellaneous savings we'd like to have on hand. It also goes for our set-and-get funds. Once we know how much we want to save and for what purposes (Christmas, vacations, new car, bigger house, and so on), we can open separate savings accounts and have them set up in the same way. As soon as our income is deposited, those amounts are automatically moved to their appropriate account. Easy-peasy.

To take it a step further, you can also automate your long-term savings for retirement in the same way. Or even better, if you have a 401(k) or traditional IRA, you can automate the amount to be deducted pretax from your salary before it even hits your bank account. You can set up the pretax deduction with your employer or human resources department directly. For a Roth IRA, you can automate a bank transfer to the fund every month; just be sure to login to your brokerage account and move the amount to your chosen investment fund (index fund, mutual fund, stock, bond, etc.).

Automation in this way sets you up for compounding advantages. It reduces decision fatigue because you only have to set them up once, it removes the amounts from your total, so you don't have to worry about overspending and not having enough to save that month, and it helps you increase your financial cushion, so you have peace of mind knowing that your financial health is stable and thriving.

Fixing your finances is a beautiful thing, and when you can take it a step further to aim your focus in the right areas, all the other little things start falling into place. When you direct your effort in the areas that have the most impact, you're essentially creating a symphony of smaller actions that work together in harmony to achieve your financial goals.

Chapter 15
Budgeting Like You Mean It

Your budget is a game changer for your financial goals. It's arguably one of the most important tools you have in your financial arsenal. It acts as a lifeline for every other area of your finances, and it's the basis of your financial health. For that reason, this entire chapter is dedicated to budgeting better so you can take control of your money and, as a result, afford more of the things that matter most to you.

It's a shame that they don't teach us how to budget in school. It's such a vital part of adulthood, and had it been taught in school, many people today would have the ability to manage their money better and consequently eliminate financial stress from their life. So, it is unfortunate that most of us didn't learn this extremely valuable skill in school.

Learn to Love Your Budget

As you've learned throughout this book, I personally hated budgeting when I first started. I viewed a budget the way a teen views their parents' house rules: It was there to take away all the fun. The idea of budgeting made me feel like I was broke and had no right to spend any of my hard-earned money. Yeah, no, thanks! I'm not voluntarily signing up for that nonsense!

Years later I'd realize that it wasn't a budget that would make me feel broke but rather my financial mindset. As I mentioned in previous chapters, I reluctantly gave in to the idea of budgeting as a last resort so we could afford to buy our house and pay off debt. And what I discovered was an entirely different reality with my budget. Here's what I realized:

- Your budget is only as restrictive as you make it. You are the creator of your budget; as such, you get to dictate where your dollars go. So if your budget feels restrictive, you have the freedom to adjust and make it so that it doesn't feel that way.

- Your budget is a snapshot of your finances. It gives you a bird's-eye view of where your money goes every month, and with that, you can spot spending leaks, plan ahead, and stay on track.
- Your budget gives you more freedom to afford the things that matter most to you. It's like a supportive assistant reminding you of your plans and helping you make the most of your income.

With your budget being such an important part of your financial health, how you create it, manage it, and adjust it matters. Budgeting isn't just about math and numbers; it's a document that encompasses your life, your goals, and your responsibilities. As such, it needs to be a living, breathing document that includes you at the core. With that said, there are some necessary steps you need to take before directing your dollars.

To understand the importance of your budget and how it enhances your life, I want to share a story that always sticks with me when I think of my categories. It's an analogy that likens your life to a jar that holds golf balls, pebbles, sand, and beer (for our purposes, we'll swap out beer for tea). Each item represents things in your life, and their size represents their importance. While the author of this thought-provoking story is still unknown, I'm thankful to have such a great visualizing tool that we can use to view our finances as well.

Let's say you have an empty jar and that represents your life. If you added golf balls all the way to the top, it would be full, right? What if you then added in small pebbles and they filled the gaps that the golf balls left, would the jar be full now? How about if you then poured in sand and it filled the even smaller gaps that the pebbles and golf balls couldn't fill, would you say the jar was full now? And what if you poured a cup of tea into the jar and it filled the even smaller space between the sand, would it now be completely full?

It's likely that your answer to each of these questions was "yes," and each time you would be correct. If this jar represents your life, the golf balls represent the truly important things—your family, children, health, friends, and favorite passions—and if everything else was lost and only they remained, your life would still be full. The pebbles are the other things that matter such as your job, home, and car. The sand represents everything else—the small stuff. If you pour the sand into the jar first, there is no room left for pebbles or golf balls. The same goes for life. If you spend all your time and energy on the small stuff, you won't have any resources left for the things that really matter to you. Pay attention to the things that are critical to your happiness, and take care of the golf balls first. Set your priorities right. Everything else is just sand. You might be wondering what the tea represents. It shows that no matter how full your life seems, there is always room for a cup of tea with a friend.

Let's now apply it to our finances.

The jar would represent our budget. The golf balls are the important categories, such as retirement savings, eliminating debt, our essential bills, emergency fund. The pebbles are other categories that matter, such as functional bills, set-and-get funds, entertainment, and personal care expenses. And the sand, the small stuff, is everything else, such as spending money on takeout, coffee runs, shopping, and so on. Tea highlights the idea that no matter how much income you have in your budget, you can always make a little room for budget-friendly fun with friends and family.

So when we think of our budget, we need to take a step back and view the entire picture. We need to see our budget as more than just a spreadsheet with numbers but rather, a plan for how we want to use our financial resources to amplify our ability to live a life we love.

In the rest of this chapter, we'll discuss how to approach your budget so that you can build the life you want with the money you have.

Prioritize You and Your Goals

Your budget needs to reflect your main goals and priorities. That should include financial cushions that help you become more financially stable, long-term savings to help you reach financial freedom and independence, and so on. It should also include your smaller but also important categories such as saving for holidays, vacations, and major purchases such as a new car or bigger home. These are your golf balls and pebbles that we talked about in the previous section, and they should be included in your budget plan first.

Be Intentional with Savings Plans

Most of us have the best of intentions when it comes to saving money. Every month we attempt to do better, save more, and spend less. But the results often don't reflect our intentions. Instead, we sometimes find ourselves over budget with no money left to save at the end of the month. That's why it's important to be intentional with your plan to save. Your savings should be looked at as a bill that you are obligated to pay. In fact, in our jar analogy, this is actually more of a baseball than a golf ball. Thus, paying yourself first by directly moving money to savings should be viewed as the most important bill you have!

When you are intentional with your savings, you can begin building the life and lifestyle you want, without taking away from any other categories. You can stop feeling guilty because you have money specifically set aside for your goals and dreams. It's one of the best feelings to know that as you save, you are essentially giving permission to yourself to enjoy your money, something we often neglect doing.

Monitor Your Expenses

Your expenses are not all created equal in importance. And many of us leave some of those expenses in our budget for far too long after their usefulness has expired. That's why a periodic review of your expenses, once every quarter or so, will be highly beneficial for your budget. Take time to assess what you pay for, what's worth your money, where you'd rather your money go, and when it's time to let go of something that isn't serving you well. This warrants repeating: In every part of your budget, look at your categories that revolve around your biggest priority, which is you.

Everything should work together to amplify your life and support your goals in the most efficient way. If an expense fails in either respect, it probably does not deserve a dollar from your resources, period. Get rid of the expense. The more you can eliminate from your budget that no longer suits your needs and your lifestyle, the better and more optimized your budget becomes. And as you declutter your financial categories by sifting through what stays and what goes, you'll inevitably clear out space and create margin in your budget plan for things that matter more. And I would argue that this is precisely when your budget transforms from a task that is dull and boring to something that gets you excited for what's to come!

Be Picky

Many of us try to squeeze as much as we can into our budget. We don't want the slightest feeling of restriction, so we think that the more we can add into our spending plan, the less restrictive it will feel. However, when we do this, it yields the completely opposite effect. Adding more restricts us rather than frees us. Let's explore why.

Because every one of us has a finite amount of financial resources, every expense we add only further depletes those limited resources. If we allow anything and everything to take our money, we'll soon find that we have no money. And that's how we start living the paycheck-to-paycheck life, not exactly the lifestyle we're hoping to achieve.

That's why it's important to be intentional with our money. When we're mindful about which things deserve our hard-earned dollars, we are forced to assess what serves us and what doesn't, and that gives us the clarity to choose only the things that are most important to us. Important items add value to your life, enhance your lifestyle, help you function better in your day-to-day, ease your stress, and ultimately give you joy.

If the things you choose to pay for don't meet these criteria, then you could be wasting valuable resources that could otherwise be used to amplify your comfort and quality of life. It's up to you to choose your expenses wisely.

Be Flexible

One of the biggest mistakes I made when I created my very first budget was being too strict. I added just bills, debt, and essential expenses only. If it wasn't something I absolutely needed, it wasn't included. I probably don't have to tell you how this turned out, but I will anyway. It was an utter failure. My budget basically expected me to go from being a spendthrift to not spending a penny outside of necessities. If I haven't said it before, I'll say it now: Cold-turkey strategies never work, at least not in the long run. They require unattainable amounts of discipline that many of us just can't sustain, not because we are lacking something but because it's a miserable way to live. What I learned is that creating a rigid budget does not magically change your habits or your lifestyle. In fact, rigidity leads to binge spending. (Yes, it's a real thing.)

Binge spending is just like it sounds. At first you try your best to conform to this crazy strict budget, and while it might work for a week, two weeks, maybe even a month, eventually you will break down and go back to your old spending urges and patterns. And that's when you'll spend more than usual, to make up for lost time and for all that deprivation you felt in the weeks you tried to keep it altogether. It's a horrible cycle that actually does more harm than good to your mindset, your behaviors, and your overall success in the long term. As a result, you develop an unhealthy relationship with your money.

Instead, create enough space and margin in your budget that gives you the flexibility to *live*. Remember how I said your budget needs to be a tool that works *with* your life? This is exactly what I meant. Your budget must have enough give to allow you to adjust and move things around as necessary. It should never be written so permanently that you can't mold it to what you need it to be. It must fit your life, not the opposite. A budget with a bit of built-in slack makes it easier to maintain long term.

Follow a Proven Framework

As you may have noticed, this chapter isn't about telling you exactly what to put in your budget. Rather, it provides a framework that guides you in creating a tailored budget that is durable enough to stand the test of time—and life, for that matter. There is no cookie-cutter method to creating a perfect budget because "perfect" is relative. Instead, these guidelines enable you to create a foundation for your budget that stabilizes your finances, maintains your spending health, and gradually begins to shift your mindset.

That is what a solid budget does. It takes your finances, in whatever state they are in now, and gives each dollar structure, direction, and purpose. And as you continue to refine it and mold it to reflect the life you want, you'll find the financial freedom you've been looking for.

Chapter 16
Let Simplicity Do the Heavy Lifting for You

"Life is really simple, but we insist on making it complicated."
—Confucius

Many people often gravitate toward complicated financial strategies, thinking those must be the most comprehensive and therefore, the best ones to apply. And those strategies almost always require a lot of discipline, a lot of effort, and generally feel challenging through and through. What's remarkable is that those very requirements, which tend to overwhelm us and cause us stress, are the very reason why we choose complexity rather than simplicity. The complex parameters give us the feeling that we're doing something important, something that takes hard work and effort to achieve. We believe that it must mean that not everyone can accomplish them, so if we succeed at them, we'll feel on top of the world.

This is likely linked to something called the "complexity bias." Complexity bias basically means that when people are faced with a choice of a complex solution or a simple one, an overwhelming majority tends to choose the complex solution.

Complex Financial Solutions Can Cost You Money

Complex strategies and solutions are often showcased in the financial space. Sadly, this is not because those complex solutions are more comprehensive or more effective. Nope, it is because complexity sells. If a company can convince you that your financial situation is complicated, then you're more likely to seek their solutions and services in order to avoid making a costly mistake. A couple of examples of this might be hiring a debt consolidation company or paying a fund manager to manage your investment portfolio. In both cases, you're convinced that properly managing finances and wealth is too complicated for an ordinary person to do well. Once you're persuaded that you aren't qualified to handle the tasks yourself, the only logical solution would be to delegate those tasks to someone more educated and qualified. What level-headed person would not want to avoid mistakes and have someone else do the heavy lifting of managing their finances? And on the surface, it might sound like a no-brainer: Take on the headache of managing it yourself or hand it off to someone else for a small fee and sit back and relax while they take care of it? Sounds reasonable and wise, so you pay someone else to do the job for you. However, the promised results almost always end up being unmet.

Let's look at debt consolidation services first. Most of those companies usually require a fee to get started and instruct you to start directing all your debt payments to them instead of sending the payments to your creditor. Meanwhile, they hold on to the money you sent and do not make payments to your creditors. This causes you to default on your debt, and your creditor will eventually sell your debt to a debt collection agency. At this point, they attempt to settle the debt for less than you originally owed. Regardless of whether they are successful in settling the debt, your credit is now undoubtedly ruined, and lenders begin to view you as a high-risk borrower, one that doesn't make good on their agreement to pay back their debt.

Similarly, a fund manager promises exceptional investment returns for your portfolio and seems to be speaking in tongues when they throw around terms such as sectors, expense ratio, securities and equities, asset allocation, and diversification strategies. All that can sound too complex for a newbie investor or an ordinary layperson to understand, let alone try to create the most optimal portfolio. Again, it seems like the obvious choice is to hand over the management of your portfolio to someone more capable who does this for a living. But most fund managers, no matter how brilliant they are, almost never beat average market returns of 7 to 10 percent per year. And if they do happen to beat those returns, their fees almost always swallow up the difference and then some. However, achieving average market returns can be as passive as investing in a low-maintenance, low-fee index fund. It doesn't require active management (hence the low-maintenance part), automatically self-cleanses, by removing companies if they drop below a certain standard, and only needs to be monitored a couple of times a year, if that. You don't need to pay a fund manager or have a degree in finance to build your financial portfolio. You are more than capable of doing it yourself and, arguably, can do it better and cheaper, to boot.

Here's the kicker. More often than not, paying for services to fix or improve your finances can do more harm than good. Hands down, you will always be more qualified and capable of being the best financial advocate for your financial well-being.

Walk, Don't Run, to Your Financial Goals

Complex financial services seem like an easy solution to your financial confusion. But simplicity can do just as much, if not more, to help you fix your finances, build your wealth, and ditch any of the financial insecurity you might be feeling. Simplicity teaches you to walk, to observe the signs, and to watch your step. You walk to make progress, observe the signs to adjust and make changes along the way, and watch your step so you avoid common pitfalls others fall into when they're hastily running.

Financial simplicity moves you to the finish line without the stress of being in the race.

Our financial journey doesn't have to be complicated to be successful. We only need to educate ourselves and trust in the process of implementing simple strategies. By reading this book, you're already taking the first step in educating yourself and reprogramming your mindset around money. Now, it's time to implement simplicity into your financial plan and trust the process.

Listen, I know how hard it can be to trust in something you've never experienced before. And on the surface, pairing simplicity with your finances may seem a bit odd. But what if simplicity is the missing piece that completely transforms your financial journey and helps you make more progress and reach success? What if it's the key to opening a world of productivity, momentum, and financial confidence? Yes, simplicity has this power.

If you allow for simplicity to be at the core of your financial plan, you'll find that it does the heavy lifting for you. It eliminates confusion and provides clarity, direction, and most of all, a straightforward path to progress. When you adopt simplicity, you are forced to break down each step into several smaller parts. That process alone helps you recognize the order of your priorities. That clarity enables you to consistently make progress without feeling stuck or overwhelmed by the task at hand so you are empowered to do more because each task feels lighter and easier to complete. You'll inevitably have more direction, so it's easier to stay on track and make steady progress toward your goals without confusion or feeling overwhelmed. One could argue that simplicity is the epitome of working smarter, not harder.

Some examples of simple steps can look like this:

- Five-minute daily budget check-in;
- Watching one YouTube video about investing in index funds;

- Eating at home one more day this week instead of paying for takeout;
- Calling your Internet provider to renegotiate your plan rate;
- Paying an extra $100 to your credit card balance this month;
- Saving $50 in your Christmas set-and-get fund;
- Opening a Roth IRA (Individual Retirement Account).

That's the beauty of simplicity: It's not about taking big leaps. It's the simple steps that allow you to take daily action, create consistency, and build momentum. That's what makes simple steps so freeing and magical. Each individual step doesn't require much time or effort, but as we saw in previous chapters, each step builds on the step before it. The compound effect can have a massive impact on your financial health and well-being.

Contrary to what many people think, simplifying your steps isn't a cop-out or a lazy approach to your finances. You aren't taking a shortcut. You're just streamlining the process to get to the same desired outcome, and that's a beautiful thing. When we can ditch the idea that anything worthwhile needs to be hard, which is often a stumbling block for our progress, we can enjoy the freedom and extra brain space that simplicity provides.

Your only challenge is trusting the process and having enough patience to see it through. Now, it can be tempting to take more than one step at a time because the steps are simpler and easier to complete. But you must resist that urge. That is the very thing that causes you to do too much too fast, and you'll find yourself overwhelmed and stressed. Openly embrace the margin of space that simple solutions add to your life. Each step is small but mighty, so let it do its job, and you'll get more done than ever before.

How Simplicity Empowers You

Let me be clear: When we simplify our steps, we tap into a powerhouse of action that creates a chain reaction that leads you to success. Your tasks become lighter and easier to accomplish. As you complete one task, you build your confidence and desire to do more. As you do more, you become consistent, and consistency creates steady progress, which continues to move you forward. It is a positive force that propels you toward reaching and crushing your financial milestones!

Simplify Your Finances, Simplify Your Life

Your finances directly impact your quality of life. When your finances feel chaotic and out of control, it can result in feelings of stress, emotional overload, and worry. Similarly, when your finances feel organized and on track, it can result in more confidence, less stress, and less worry. Simplicity allows you to better manage your finances so that you can have the financial freedom to afford a life you love. It also lightens your financial burden as you begin to consistently take steps that provide more breathing room for your money.

Simplicity Gets Rid of Barriers

Up until this point, your financial journey may have felt like a series of obstacles that you have to overcome. It can feel stressful, overwhelming, and sometimes frustrating. But our finances were never meant to create problems for us to solve. Our financial path is meant to help us manage our resources in a way that enables us to achieve our dream life, one that brings us joy and makes us feel fulfilled and content.

Simplifying your financial systems takes away the barriers that would stop you in your tracks and helps you move forward more consistently, without hesitation. Every step becomes easy enough to take the necessary action without second-guessing yourself. That alone can help you accomplish milestones faster, and you can achieve your goals in less time.

Simplicity Declutters Your Finances

If you were to declutter your closet, you'd probably have more space, better organization, and a lot of freedom. Likewise, our financial portfolio (the metaphorical closet that houses our finances) needs decluttering from time to time as well. Simplicity is the process that makes it possible to declutter and get rid of the space wasters in your financial closet.

When you simplify your budget, for example, you will remove the items that take up valuable financial resources and no longer serve you. You'll keep only those line items that serve a purpose in your current season of life and items that bring you joy. As you declutter, you give yourself the opportunity to assess and adjust as needed. Simplifying your financial systems allows you to eliminate and reorganize tasks so you can better optimize your to-do list. That ultimately gives you more space to breathe, think, and take better action.

Simplicity Builds Healthy Financial Habits

Simplicity creates solid habits that become ingrained in the routines of your daily life. You can rely on these habits to consistently support your progress even during tougher days when you're not feeling motivated to get things done. That's because simplicity is subtle, easy, and doesn't disrupt your life in order to create change.

Keeping it simple helps you create a better relationship with your money. As you take each small step, you build momentum, confidence, and better control of your money. That foundation helps you build better money habits. And those healthy habits turn into systems and routines that help you manage your money well in both the short term and long term.

Simplicity Amplifies Progress

By far, one of my favorite benefits of simplifying your finances is the ability to amplify your progress without running faster or doing more. With clear direction and better focus, you'll get much more done than if you were faced with complicated tasks. You no longer procrastinate because the simple steps removed the intimidation you used to feel. Simplicity gives you confidence to take each step without hesitation, and as a result, you can get more done than ever before.

Secrets to Becoming a Saving Whiz, Unlocked

Congratulations! You have made it to the end of this chapter and the entire book! Along the way, we talked about the magic of small steps, trusting the process, the importance of patience and consistency, practical applications to help you save and become savvier with your money, and much more. While all the topics we discussed in this book are vital to your financial success and sustainability, simplicity is the nucleus that holds it altogether. In my own life, I heavily rely on simplicity to do my heavy lifting, so I know just how transformative it can be if you let it work for you. I urge you to ditch the desire to make big moves all at once and instead make those moves using smaller steps. You owe it to yourself and your financial health to operate from a place that provides enough margin to breathe, think, and assess with more intention. Simplifying your plan removes the busy work and helps you implement impactful steps that move you forward. With every step you complete, you'll free up more time and energy to do more of the things you love and enjoy. It's in the simple steps that you find the most clarity and financial confidence to afford a life you love.

Now go out there, take one step forward, and begin your money journey with confidence. You've got this!

About the Author

Gina Zakaria is a personal finance educator with more than 5 million followers on social media, a savings expert, and the founder of Saving Whiz, a money education platform where she shares simple strategies to help women take charge of their finances the easy way. Through her small-step approach, she breaks down complex money topics into simple, actionable steps that empower women (and some men) to make financial progress. Gina is passionate about teaching others how to comfortably maximize on life while saving money. Gina has been in the money space for more than 20 years and has been featured in *Forbes*, *Money Magazine*, *Good Morning America*, *NBC Today*, and other prominent personal finance sites. Her approach of simplicity and small, gradual steps has been embraced by people around the world to help them transform their lives.

Index

C

D